HOW TO BECOME A SUCCESSFUL FREELANCE TRANSLATOR

Earning an income from home as a translator

by Françoise Jefferies MCIL
www.strictlyfrench.co.uk

ISBN: 978-1-910662-27-4

First published in 2016

A BIT ABOUT ME

I grew up in France and from my first day at secondary school, I found foreign languages exciting and fun to learn. But back then I hadn't thought about studying languages to a high level and I had no idea that one day I would be multilingual and make a living out of speaking and writing in different languages.

As a starting note, I want to stress that I didn't grow up bilingual, nor did I have the opportunity to travel when I was younger. I just eagerly learned the two foreign languages (English and German) that I had the opportunity to study at secondary school and, because I enjoyed them so much, spent many hours in my spare time concentrating on what to me was a pleasurable activity and therefore didn't feel like an effort.

I loved languages so much so that I took up a third one (Spanish) for my Baccalauréat exam (A level equivalent in France). Once I passed, I took a year out to go to Germany in order to experience living in another country and speaking a foreign language. To me travelling, living abroad and immersing myself in a foreign culture were all the right ingredients for the best possible adventure, one I found thoroughly exciting.

Back in France, I completed a two year language and business studies course which enabled me to extend my language skills and at the end of the course I was ready to start work doing what I loved best: using languages. Through my studies, I had the opportunity to do a short placement at Siemens, in Germany, and ended up staying 5 years before deciding that I wanted to move to London.

My early career

For the first 15 years of my career, I held office based jobs making full use of my language skills in different roles as a trilingual personal assistant and conference organiser for several blue chip companies. In that sense, I can say that translating has always been part of my job and my experience as a translator stretches back to my first day at work. I was often told at work that I had a gift for translating and I became gradually aware that this might indeed be a special skill I had. Years later, when I decided to stay at home due to family commitments, becoming a translator became an obvious career choice.

My journey to becoming a freelance translator

I found the transition from being employed to working as a freelance translator unsettling, partly because I had no formal qualifications as a translator and I had no support whatsoever around me. Through personal contacts, I was offered the opportunity to translate some documents on an ad hoc basis. Though I should have relished such an opportunity, I was actually uncomfortable for several reasons:

- Despite my experience and high level of language capability, I didn't have any formal qualifications as a translator and I didn't like being in that situation. Part of me felt almost like a fraud and not knowing exactly where I stood made me feel unsure about the quality of my work.

- By then I had been living outside France for a number of years and my exposure to the French language – or lack of it – meant that I didn't feel proficient anymore in my own language! Words I hadn't heard for a long time didn't come easily to my mind. This might seem odd, but you can actually lose your skills in your mother tongue, just as you can in a foreign language, if you stop practising for a long period of time!

- The documents I was translating were of a technical nature and I was quite unfamiliar with the subject matter. Under such circumstances, it is easy to feel intimidated and although I managed to perform satisfactorily, I probably worked way too hard to try and produce what I perceived as being an acceptable level of translation. When I was given feedback and saw the corrections made to my text, this was again a source of anxiety for me and convinced me even more of my shortcomings. I know now that this is a normal part of the translation process and some reviewers do make an excessive number of changes, which may have nothing to do with the quality of the translation.

- I didn't have all the help I needed at my fingertips and was inexperienced in researching words, phrases or specialist subject matters. Now there is an abundance of help which is easy and quick to access and I feel confident enough to translate a semi-technical text on subjects I didn't even know existed before!

For all the above reasons, I decided that my next step would be to obtain a formal qualification as a translator.

I decided to take the Diploma in Translation exam of the Institute of Linguists (now called the Chartered Institute of Linguists). I contacted a university who was offering a distance learning course in preparation for the exam and was sent a past paper to translate as a test before being accepted on the course. I found the test challenging and it was a nerve-wracking wait until I got confirmation that I had the required level to be taken on the course.

The next 12 months were spent preparing for the exam, not just by doing past papers and having them marked and annotated by a tutor, but by reading the theory of translation. I bought a book called 'La Traduction Raisonnée', which turned out to be immensely valuable. It made me see my mother tongue in ways I had never been made aware of before and, as I worked my way through the book, I was able to access another level of my own language, spot challenges and recognise how to deal with them when translating. It gave me confidence. This is precisely what I felt I was missing when I started translating without any training.

When the day of the exam arrived, I was as prepared as I could have been and took the three papers (seven hours in total) with relative ease. When I received the results in the post a few weeks later, there was a disconcerting moment when the result sheet showed a D next to the two semi-specialised papers and it took me a while to work out that D actually stood for Distinction and that I had successfully passed everything!

Having achieved the Diploma in Translation of the Institute of Linguists, I started contacting translation agencies and soon got my first job. From then on I gradually increased my workload by signing up with more agencies, until I ultimately got enough work directly from clients. I became a qualified translator in 2003 and looking back, the change of career I made is one that has served me well and I am still very happy about today.

WHO THIS BOOK IS FOR

If you are fluent in two or more languages with a high standard of written language in your mother tongue and you find the prospect of working from home appealing for any of the following reasons then this book will show you what steps to take in order to become a successful freelance translator:

- you love the idea of working from the comfort of your own home
- you love the idea of working from anywhere in the world and earning an income by just having your laptop with you
- you have a young family and you want to stay at home while at the same time earn an income
- you are a carer for a member of your family and you need to be home based
- you have an office job but you would like the flexibility of working from home
- you want to work from home because of any other personal reason or circumstance

Purpose of this book and how it will benefit you

In this book, I share my experience of becoming and working as a freelance translator. I retrace the steps I have taken to be where I am today and explain what options are available to anyone who, like me, is passionate about languages and would love to work from home as a translator. I also explain what I have learnt along the way and what additional skills are needed other than being good at languages.

Once you have read the book and absorbed its content, you will know what to do in order to:

- qualify as a translator
- get the essential equipment you need to get started
- apply for jobs and start working, even with little or no experience
- keep abreast of changes and work on your continuous professional development
- fast track yourself into a career as a freelance translator

I will also

- tell you what the industry of freelance translation feels like
- make you aware of the pros and cons of embarking on a career as a freelance translator
- give you personal examples of what I have learnt along the way.

CONCLUSION

With this book my aim is to help you make a clear and informed choice and to reach your goal faster. I have provided many real life examples as this is the best way to show you what it feels like to work as a freelance translator.

This book is written from my own personal experience being based in the UK. However, the lessons, tips and ideas, can of course be applied anywhere. Where UK organisations or references are given, the equivalent will exist in your country of residence. In addition, this is a profession without borders and your geographical location, except for tax and legislation, is largely irrelevant.

CONTENTS

Chapter 1

SUPPLY AND DEMAND: WILL I MAKE MONEY?

Deciding to become a freelance translator

After I had decided to train as a translator, it was another year before I took the plunge and signed up for a course. Despite my educational and professional background, I wasn't at all confident that I had the required skill level to translate professionally and I kept putting the decision off. With hindsight, I should have trusted my instinct and not hesitated so much.

If you love languages and you find the prospect of using them to earn a living from home exciting, you probably inherently know that you have what it takes to become a professional freelance translator. Although it is natural to have some doubt, I would encourage anyone reading this book to trust themselves and embrace your new career choice, if you feel that this is something you would truly love.

Is there work as a translator?

Towards the end of my one year distance learning translation course I remember asking my tutor whether there was work in the translating sector and she assured me that there was. Although this was over ten years ago, demand for translation services, especially for technical translations, is stronger than ever and on the increase.

The globalisation of commerce and the development of digital communications mean that a lot of small companies are now able to compete in international markets and find that they need to speak their customers' language in order to reach them more effectively. More and more sophisticated products are being manufactured and existing products are often equipped with additional features. This means that a lot of technical documentation must be produced, updated and translated into the end users' languages. In larger companies, legislation and the desire to communicate clearly often require that internal communications to employees be translated into the language of the country a company is operating in. According to the UNESCO Institute for Statistics, the adult literacy rate has been increasing over the past two decades and this trend contributes in the long run to more exchanges between people and countries, fuelling the need for translation services. All these factors support the idea that demand for translation services will continue to grow in the foreseeable future.

In addition, despite the prevalence of English in business, it is important and even essential for many companies to translate their literature into local languages to give their customers a better experience and have a stronger impact in smaller communities. Even international groups advertise and pride themselves in having a global reach with a local touch.

Will working as a freelance translator make you rich?

Knowing how much you will earn as a freelance translator would obviously help your motivation and decision making. However, there is no quick and easy answer to this question, as it depends on several factors and circumstances. Your ability to earn a living from translating will develop over time as you get more established. Therefore, as in any profession, your earning potential will be different at the start than further down your career path. Having said that, it is fair to want to know if working as a translator will give you a good income. So, simply put: will it make you rich?

If 'rich' means the type of income that's typical of a high pressured, fast paced environment, then the answer is no. When you choose to become a freelance translator, it is because you want to earn a living by doing a job you are passionate about and will enjoy, a job that will give you a lot of satisfaction because it enables you to have an interesting and stimulating activity, which offers flexibility and a good work-life balance.

TOP TIP

Remember to take into consideration that it will take time for you to build up a sustainable, decent income from this profession. Go into it with your long term future at the forefront of your mind and you will have a better chance of succeeding.

How much you will earn will depend on several factors:

- **The volume of work that you will be able to take on**

  As you are most likely to charge according to the number of words, the more you translate, the more you will earn.

- **Your language pair, which are the two languages between which you translate**

  The rarer and more sought after your language pair, the higher the rates you will be able to negotiate.

- **Whether you work for clients directly or through agencies**

  Agencies can take up to 40% commission, so it is more lucrative to find your own clients and work with them directly. However it is easier to start working through agencies if you have limited experience.

- **Your specialist subjects**

  The more specialised you are, the less competition you will have and the more you will be able to charge. This is also determined by who you are working for: is it a business with a lot of resources and tight deadlines, or is it a small company or organisation with limited resources?

- **Quality versus quantity**

  It is quality which will determine the rate you charge and your volume of work over time. When you start working regularly on a specific subject, you deepen your knowledge through the research you do around each translation assignment, and that experience eventually turns you into a specialist in that particular subject. Your knowledge makes you more valuable to your clients because they know that your work is of a high standard and they can trust you. If you don't specialise, you will be competing on price and that tends to drag the rates down. So the choice is: quality at a higher rate or volume at a lower rate.

- **Your own standards and work ethic**

  You might sometimes think that you are spending too much time working on a text but ultimately it always pays off. Your drive for perfection is what your clients value and what sets you apart from the competition. It is precisely this quality which affords you the luxury of competing on elements other than price. This attitude will ensure that you attract work that pays a decent rate. Once your clients are impressed by the quality and speed of your work, the care and attention to detail as well as your responsiveness and reliability, you will become extremely valuable to them. Not only will they keep coming back to you, but you will be able to put your rate up. This in turn enables you to earn more and once you have sufficient work you can afford to set the rate you are comfortable with, so it becomes a virtuous circle.

- **Your experience**

  At the beginning of your new career, you will almost certainly find yourself working part time because you need to build up your contacts until you have sufficient work. For this reason, a lot of translators start by working through agencies, as it seems to be the easiest and quickest way to get off the ground.

  Over time, having gained more experience and confidence, you will be able to take on work with direct clients. When you do extensive work for individual companies, you become proficient in matters relating to their industry. This enables you to create your own niche and market your newly acquired specialist skills to prospective clients.

CONCLUSION

Working as a translator is not a gateway to a get-rich-quick scheme, but it delivers a good income once you are established and a high level of job satisfaction. If you value being based at home while being part of a professional community (more on this later), having flexible hours and being stimulated with linguistic challenges on a daily basis, translation lets you determine a work-life balance that suits you exactly.

In the next chapter I am going to discuss the importance of training and gaining a formal qualification as a freelance translator.

Chapter 2

DO I NEED TO TRAIN TO BECOME A FREELANCE TRANSLATOR?

Of course it is possible to work as a translator without formal qualifications. However, it is much harder to get work in a competitive market place if you can't show some proficiency. Unless you have exceptional skills and a proven track record in translation work, you will find it useful to have a recognised qualification when you apply for jobs. Although it might take you several months to a year to prepare, this is a valuable investment into your future, not to mention a stimulating and enjoyable learning process.

Advantages of a formal qualification

Gaining a formal qualification will make the job easier in several respects:

- It will give you credibility. Potential clients will relate to you differently as they will recognise your qualifications and this will enable you to have a different conversation with them at the start of a relationship and when you discuss a potential job and talk about your rates.

- You will be more competitive. I remember applying to translate documents on sea defences with a company specialised in marine equipment. Also competing for the job was an engineer with years of experience in the industry but no qualifications as a translator. As a test translation, we were given a sample of the project which was very technical and therefore a huge challenge to me. Despite this, I decided not to work too hard on it: I didn't want to win a job that was above my ability and which would require me to work extraordinarily hard at every step. To my surprise, I won the contract and this gave me several weeks' work. The translation didn't prove as hard as I had first feared and this job gave me the opportunity to expand into an area I knew nothing about previously.

- You will be more able to tackle a document and do a better job because you will have learnt to spot linguistic challenges and you will know how to deal with them.
- You will have more confidence in yourself and your work will be more enjoyable as you won't worry about missing something or being substandard.
- You will be able to work more quickly because you will have honed your language skills and learnt techniques to make you more proficient.

An example of getting a professional qualification

Tho Diploma in Translation from the Chartered Institute of Linguists (CIOL) -

The CIOL is a UK-based body of professional linguists working in a wide range of disciplines, from translators and interpreters to language teachers, university lecturers and linguists, who use their foreign language skills in business, the professions and government. It offers a range of fully accredited professional qualifications for linguists which are recognised by government departments, agencies, business organisations, universities and schools. It also lists on its website a number of course providers with their contact details and the languages in which the courses are offered in the UK and 13 other countries. You can then find the course that will help you prepare for the Diploma in Translation examination and contact the course provider directly for more costs, starting date and more details.

How much will it cost to train as a professional translator?*

The Diploma in Translation from the Chartered Institute of Linguists consists of three papers and carries an exam fee of £400 for the main paper and £298 for each of the two semi-specialised papers, although you can choose to take all three for a total of £595. There is also a fee of £51 per paper for taking the exam. On top of that, you might decide that you need a course to prepare for the exam. As an example, a 10 week course at a Further Education College will cost you around £600. In addition, you might want to invest in some books on the theory of translation and possibly buy some dictionaries, although this might not be necessary until you start working in a specialised area. In total, this means that you can be a fully qualified translator within about a year for around £1,500. I would say this is reasonable in terms of time frame and outlay for a whole new career, especially if you are already in a job and you can carry on working while you study for the course. So overall, getting a professional qualification as a translator doesn't have to take years, and it doesn't have to be a huge expense.

* *prices correct at time of going to press.*

Steps towards training to become a professional translator

1. Assess your language skills

The first thing to do is decide whether your language level and writing skills are sufficient to join a course. Consider the following:

- Your source language (that's the language you intend to translate from): how fluent are you in it? Do you understand the finest nuances in a text?

- Your target language (that's the language you want to translate into, normally your mother tongue): do you write it with perfect grammar and spelling? Can you articulate the slightest nuances in that language? Are you skilled at formulating your thoughts and ideas? Do you take pride in the way you write? Do people tell you that you have a gift when it comes to putting something in writing?

Once you have checked your language competence, you should look for a course that will prepare you to pass an examination leading to a formal qualification as a translator or at the very least attempt some past papers and read about translation theory.

If you have a higher education such as a degree, or if writing is part of your job then you know that you are likely to have the required skill level. If you apply for a translation course, the course provider should ask you to do a test translation, such as a past exam paper and that will confirm whether your level of language is sufficient to consider training.

2. Find a course that will prepare you for your professional examination

Although you can attempt the Diploma in Translation or another formal qualification without going on a course, I found it very useful to familiarise myself with the skill level that was required, learn exam techniques, do past papers within real exam conditions and have an experienced translator as a tutor who corrected my work and gave me precious feedback.

Personally I signed up with Bracknell and Wokingham Further Education College. This was a 12 month distance learning course whereby I used to receive and translate past exam papers and e-mail them to a tutor, who would send them back with corrections and annotations. I also had several conversations over the phone with my tutor, which was part of the course. I purchased additional papers and examiner's reports and this enabled me to do extra work on top of the one year course. Although these extra papers didn't get corrected, I found the examiner's report on them very useful as it mentioned mistakes frequently made by candidates and had pointers on how to produce a better translation. During those 12 months I did about 40 different papers, which meant that I was extremely familiar with the technique by the time my course ended and I was ready and prepared to take the exam.

3. Read on the theory

Once you have selected a course provider and signed up, you will be given a lot of practical advice including which books to read to make the most of your studies. You will learn exam techniques and how to deal with tricky idioms and phrases. I found reading on the theory not just invaluable but fascinating. Although I did a lot of past papers, it wasn't the sheer amount of work alone that enabled me to make huge progress, but the fact that I was gaining a sharper understanding of structures within my language pair.

4. Get up to speed on language and cultural development

When I started my course I suddenly became aware of how rusty my French had become. I had been working in an English speaking environment for years and was only using French in private conversations. I wasn't keeping myself informed on what was going on in France and found there were a lot of new words linked to technology and lifestyle aspects. There were also words and phrases I hadn't heard for years and couldn't recall as easily as I used to. What's more, some definitions became fuzzy in my mind and I wasn't always sure about the full extent of their meaning in any given context. I became aware that I needed to brush up on my mother tongue!

5. Listen to the radio

At that point I decided to start listening to the radio and this is something I highly recommend. I was fortunate enough to pick up France Inter, which is a state run radio station of very high quality (similar to Radio Four in the UK) with news, political debates, cultural programmes, etc. There was always something interesting to listen to no matter what time of the day I tuned in. The major advantage of listening to the radio, of course, is that it allows you to get on with a lot of other tasks, provided they don't demand your full attention. I bought a small portable radio and started carrying it with me around the house and even listening to it at night time with an earpiece. I am now at a stage when it is second nature to me and I even have to consciously cut back. However, this has proved absolutely invaluable to bring my French back up to the level I wanted. Now of course, this option is even more easily available to anyone through the Internet. You can get as many as 8,000 different stations from around the world through an internet radio, so you are almost certain to find an interesting foreign language channel. If you are short of time or need to be on the move, listening to the radio or to podcasts is a great way of using the time you have to bring your language up to speed.

6. Watch TV

Watching television to improve your language skills offers all the benefits of listening to the radio but is obviously more time consuming. However, if you can afford to sit down and watch some programmes, or if you are able to get on with your day while having the television on, this is extremely beneficial. Some people prefer to absorb information through a combination of sight and sound. Having subtitles on the screen can also be useful.

7. Read up on subjects you are interested in working in

If there is one particular topic you are interested in working in, try and read as widely on the subject matter as you can. That way you will work on your language and build some expertise in what can become your niche at the same time. You might have specialist knowledge in a particular area from your current job or an earlier career, so even without much experience as a translator, you will have a head start over other translators. Depending on your chosen subject or discipline, you can deepen your knowledge by going a step further through magazine subscriptions, visits to trade shows and conferences. All these are ways of gathering experience and credibility before you are even ready to apply for work.

CONCLUSION

Once you have decided that working as a freelance translator is the right choice of career for you, take all the necessary steps that will help you assess your skills and decide what action you need to take to give yourself the best chances to succeed. Take seriously the need to maintain and develop your knowledge of and interest in your chosen language pair. Personally, I recommend working for a professional qualification. I believe that the effort you put in is part of your investment in a career you will love and that will serve you well.

So now you have thought about the practical skills you will need, there is another side to consider on your journey. In the next chapter, I will be talking about some of the issues a translator can come across and how to deal with them.

Chapter 3

GETTING STARTED: COMMON PROBLEMS AND POSSIBLE SOLUTIONS

This chapter reveals some highs and lows of the profession and how to deal with them to help you think through if you are a translator at heart. It also outlines other non-language related skills that are essential to be successful as a translator.

As you embark on your new career, you will encounter some issues, both emotional and practical. Your responses will depend, of course, on your own personal experiences and attitude. These are the main issues I encountered and some tips on how to deal with them.

Issue 1: you might feel on your own

At times, especially at the beginning of your new career, you might find it unsettling to suddenly be on your own and responsible for every aspect of getting your career off the ground. This is especially the case if previously you have always been in paid employment. You might have questions about promoting yourself, what rate to charge and how to negotiate with potential clients. You might feel overwhelmed as you need to market your services, do administration work and sort out your taxes, for example – all while you are translating.

What you can do:

- **Contact other translators you know**

The first thing I did after qualifying was to contact two translators I knew personally and sit down with them with a list of questions on how to get started. They gave me valuable information and showed me practical steps to actually get going. If you know a translator, I suggest you contact them. I was grateful for their help and I have, in turn, given advice to newly qualified translators. This is also the reason for this book and why I have tried to make it as practical as possible, and based on experience.

- **Join a translators' forum**

If you have passed the Diploma in Translation of the Institute of Linguists, you will be able to join Transnet, the Institute's online translators' forum which is very active and very helpful. You can post questions if you find a word or phrase particularly challenging, get technical advice if you have a problem with your hardware or software and find out through other members whether a particular agency is reputable and honest. On top of the general forum, other groups have been set up within Transnet for specific languages such as French, Arabic, etc. Depending on your language pair, you can post questions directly to the relevant group, to translators who work in the same languages as you. Even when you haven't got questions or don't need help, you can follow exchanges between translators and access a wealth of information on useful links, events, advice on online dictionaries, terminology, what computer or software to buy, and more. There are also frequent posts warning you of possible scams, a subject I will discuss in detail in Chapter 11.

- **Become a member of a translators' association**

The Institute of Translation & Interpreting (ITI) is an association for practising translation and interpreting professionals which offers various membership categories from fellows to students, so you can join even if you have not yet qualified. The association offers a range of benefits to all its members including networking opportunities, access to job adverts, free use of a credit checking facility for UK businesses and a free payment irregularities reporting tool. For full details visit the ITI website on www.iti.org.uk.

- **Sign up to a membership-based website for translators**

Some of the best known membership-based sites are: Proz, TranslatorsCafé, TranslationDirectory, TraduGuide.com and TranslatorsBase. These are websites used by translators to find job offers. You can sign up to these websites and bid for projects which are offered. Many companies and agencies post translation jobs on these sites to which anyone can apply. I know a translator who received a job offer the very day she joined and hasn't stopped working since! These websites are open to anyone and you don't need proof of qualification, but please remember that you are potentially competing against many applicants from all over the world. Rates can be fairly low but these sites are still a useful place to get started when you want to earn an income and build up some experience.

Issue 2: you might feel stuck with an IT problem

When you work for yourself, you might find yourself stuck because of a technical problem with your hardware or software and you don't have any technical support around you. Unless you have a close friend or relative who is an IT expert, you feel that your only option is to pay for a professional to help you out.

What you can do:

- **Post a question on a translators' forum**

This is where, once again, being part of a community of translators, such as an online forum, enables you to find a lot of the answers you are looking for. You will find that some of the members are technically very proficient and will often be able to help you solve your problem.

- **Do some research online**

Although this might be time consuming just when you are in the middle of a job and you feel you need to get on with your work quickly, the solution might be simpler than you think. Unless you are working to a tight deadline, treat this as an exercise in the acquisition of new skills. If you find the solution by yourself, you will have the satisfaction of having gained some knowledge and solved a problem and you will feel more empowered and more confident.

- **Contact a student**

If you need some professional help, why not first contact a student who is proficient in computing but won't cost as much as a professional IT consultant. You might have personal contacts to highly computer literate pupils or students. Alternatively, you can contact a website such as www.studentgems.com which puts students and professionals in touch for odd jobs in many areas including IT. The students are very proficient in the skills they advertise and they normally charge about half what a professional would. They are very keen to build up a portfolio of work that will demonstrate their experience as well as earn some money and most of them are eager to do a good job.

- **Get help from a professional IT consultant**

If the problem is bigger than you thought and everything else has failed, find a professional IT consultant, preferably through a recommendation, and if you are pleased with their service, keep their details as you might need them again in future. Treat the expense as an inevitable cost that is part of business life and bear in mind that this is a cost you can offset against your income tax, so don't forget to ask for an invoice before they leave.

Issue 3: you might feel socially isolated

It can sometimes feel hard not to have any colleagues around to help and support and share what you are going through, or just for company. When you feel isolated, remember that thousands of people who go to an office everyday dream of swapping their commute and their many sources of stress for the kind of work environment that you are enjoying. It is normal, however, to wish from time to time that you had a more established work structure with guaranteed interaction with other professionals and like-minded people.

What you can do:

- **Join a forum (see Issue 1 above)**

Being in touch with other translators through a forum creates a whole community around you. The exchanges don't have to be limited to discussions around problems and solutions, but can also revolve around wider issues. For example, for discussions on non-language topics, the Chartered Institute of Linguists' forum, Transnet, has a virtual place called the Winebar, where translators can chat freely on other topics. Often language related topics get moved from Transnet to the Winebar after a while, once the issue in question has been answered and some people feel like digressing and adding personal stories or moving away from the subject altogether. This avoids distracting those translators who are under pressure to carry on working and doesn't clog up the forum and those with time on their hands can carry on the online conversation.

- **Attend events**

Of course, joining a forum means that interactions with others are still virtual and this doesn't replace physical contact, but you can go beyond the Internet. Events organised by the Chartered Institute of Linguists, the ITI or Proz enable members to meet up at conferences, on cultural visits and courses, giving the opportunity to make new contacts and get together with some of the people they communicate with online.

- **Find out if there is a translator's social group in your area**

Some translators use their forum to organise local get-togethers for members who live in the same area. When you join a forum, find out whether such a group exists near you, and if not, why not take the initiative and create one.

- **Meet with your friends and other professionals**

Being based at home gives you the flexibility to meet people during the day and this is something people working away full time can only dream of. You can organise your time and working hours to ensure that, from time to time at least, you see some of your friends or take part in courses, activities or social events you are interested in. These don't always have to be related to your work nor do they need to occur on a weekly basis but taking part will break your routine and give you that extra dimension which makes working from home more enjoyable.

Issue 4: you might feel unsure about your skills

You might have some doubt about your skills and abilities. This is particularly true at the beginning of your career when you have limited experience and you might be unsure about how to deal with clients. With every job you do and every piece of great feedback you receive from your clients, you feel your confidence grow and you think that you have reached a stage where you are able to tackle anything. However, even further down the line your confidence can get knocked. I have been working as a translator for over 15 years and I sometimes find myself, even now, doubting whether I have done a good job, especially when I receive changes to be implemented.

What you can do

- **Keep your perspective**

Remind yourself of your natural ability and passion for languages. You know that you can work to a high standard. Every translator occasionally encounters challenging and even daunting tasks. The secret is to assess a job carefully before accepting it and not to take anything which is beyond your ability.

- **Learn from mistakes**

Your first draft might need a lot of rework, but this is also what makes your job stimulating. You want to be stretched and apply your skills to arrive at a beautiful result in the same way a craftsman produces a beautiful object to be proud of. Every challenge is an opportunity to improve and improvement leads to greater confidence.

- **Allow more time, especially at the beginning**

If you haven't got a lot of experience, it might be a good idea to negotiate a deadline which leaves you with a comfortable amount of time to do the work. If the subject is unfamiliar or you struggle with writing, you will need to go over your work more times than a more experienced translator and maybe research some words and phrases. Some jobs will feel like they are not worth the time you spend on them, but with hindsight you will find that they all contribute to improve not just your skills but also your reputation, so never give up.

- **Follow discussions on forums**

When you read language queries other translators post on forums, it makes you realise that no one has all the answers. Often, there isn't a set way of translating a phrase or sentence and this is where translators need to be creative, follow their instinct and sometimes their preference. The suggestions posted by other translators often show that the language needs to be adapted and your ideas can be as valid as anyone else's. You might even be able to post an answer and help a fellow translator find a solution!

- **Consider further training**

If you think you might benefit from learning about a specific subject or translation techniques, find out a suitable course and sign up. In pretty much any job nowadays, you need to keep your skills up to date and to the required level, so consider this to be an investment into your future. Perfect your skills or acquire the qualifications that will help you further yourself in your career.

- **Start part-time while still working elsewhere**

If you are in paid employment and you are concerned about leaving your job to be a freelance translator in case it doesn't work out, a good alternative is to start small by doing translation work part-time. There is no substitute for trying it out and once you know what it feels like to do a piece of work, deliver it and get feedback on it, you will know whether this is something you want to do as your main job.

Issue 5: you might sometimes feel discouraged

There will be days when you wish you could do something else instead. Sometimes a translation job proves harder than you thought and you don't enjoy it; you are not happy about the time you spend on it and you start to think you wish you were doing something else for a living. This might just be a sign that you are overworked.

What you can do

Whenever I have felt this way about my job, I have found the simplest solution the best: take a break, whether for 15 minutes or a week. I have come back refreshed, looking forward to receiving the next job and ready to start again with renewed enthusiasm and energy. Sometimes it is easy to overlook the fact that translation is an intellectually stimulating activity which gives you a lot of flexibility, a nice work-life balance and enjoyable challenges. Remember, many paid jobs turn out to be very tedious and boring and don't give people the opportunity to do anything about it. As a freelance translator, you have, to a certain extent, the luxury of being able to accept a job or turn it down if it doesn't appeal to you.

TOP TIP

As a freelance translator, you are on your own and therefore your first and most important step is to seek a community of other professionals in order to get the support you need and the information that will help you get off the ground and flourish.

CONCLUSION

When you start working as a freelance translator, you will be experience an emotional roller coaster. You might take this journey in your stride or find it challenging, depending how prepared you are. What I have described in this chapter are some of the personal experiences I went through in an attempt to give you an insight into the daily work of a freelance translator and help you decide whether this environment would be appealing to you and suit your personality. Obviously, only you can answer that question.

The main point is: every job has its ups and downs and the difficulties I have outlined can all be overcome, so don't let them hinder you.

For myself, having occasionally, fleetingly considered switching to another job, I have always come to the conclusion that there is no better job in the world than being a freelance translator because of the stimulating work, the thrill of getting it just right and the flexibility and freedom it gives you to organise your time as you wish. And this is when you know that you are a translator at heart.

In the next chapter, I will be reviewing the various sources of work you can explore when you are ready to start your new career.

Chapter 4

HOW TO FIND WORK AS A FREELANCE TRANSLATOR

You are all set up and ready to go. All you need now is your first translation assignment! For this to happen, you will have to let potential customers know that you are available. When they do find you, you will need to convince them that you are the right person for their translation requirement and make them want to give you the job. This chapter explores ways to market yourself to get your first paid project.

A simple start: credentials

To begin with, prepare a credentials document introducing yourself and your services. This needs to be clear and to the point, showing your skills, qualifications and relevant experience. See Chapter 8 for more information on how to draw up a CV and personal profiles. This exercise will help you express clearly what you are offering.

SOURCES OF WORK

There are a number of different sources of work you can explore when you start looking for your first job and you will find a list of them below. It is a good idea to pursue several avenues simultaneously in order to give yourself the best chance of finding work as soon as possible.

1. Translation agencies

Contacting translation agencies is one of the most obvious first steps and a lot of new translators start here. First of all, identify potential agencies which match your language pair and specialisms. Have a look at their websites to find out what area they specialise in (e.g. there is no point applying to an agency which only uses translators with a scientific or legal background if your speciality is business and marketing).

Be clear and concise

Once you have selected suitable agencies, send them a short e-mail, making it clear in the subject line that you are applying for work and state your language pair. By being clear and concise, you will save them time and you will have a better chance of having your application taken into consideration. Agencies are busy and receive many applications. If they have to look hard to determine your profile and find out what you are offering, they may not bother.

In the body of your message, explain briefly what your specialist areas are if you have any, what major work you have done and, if relevant what other services you offer such as transcription, proofreading, etc. (more on this in Chapter 10). Then attach your credentials and send your application. Bear in mind that your grammar and spelling must be absolutely perfect as your application serves to demonstrate how professional you are. I would encourage you to contact as many suitable agencies as possible, although this is best done over a period of time to give yourself the chance to learn from the process at every step.

Agencies like to receive applications which are short and straight to the point. Only mention experience which is relevant to the services you are offering and present it clearly. According to some agencies a surprisingly high number of translators forget to state their language pair!

Test market your applications

The effectiveness of your e-mail applications will depend on several factors including your subject line. Don't just send identical applications that are all worded in the same way to all your prospective clients. Instead, tailor your applications, keep refining them and see what works best. As well as varying your subject lines, you could word the body of your message in a more conservative style for some of your applications and opt for a more aggressive selling stance in some others.

It is usually accepted amongst translators that the response rate from agencies ranges between 5% and 10%. Out of those who respond, you can expect up to 5% to put you on their books and between 2% and 5% to actually send you some work. To a certain extent, you can say it's a numbers game. This being the case, the best thing to do is simply to get started; plough your way through lots of applications and look forward to those positive responses that will materialise sooner or later.

Don't be too concerned by your lack of experience, rather concentrate on what you have to offer: have you got qualifications showing your language proficiency? Have you got knowledge in a specialist subject from a previous job? Agencies may be contacted by many applicants every day but not all applications are of good quality and even the good people on their books move on. So don't be defeated and keep believing in yourself.

Explore as many sources of work as you can and do not be disheartened by a low response rate. Most translators experience this when they start out. Remember that this doesn't reflect on you in any way and it takes time and effort to get that first door to open.

Stand out from the crowd with a flexible attitude

You can easily stand out in several ways to give yourself the edge:

- Be responsive and accept a job that is urgent – provided, of course, that it is within your ability and you can deliver quality. This sometimes involves making a quick decision and setting all other plans and priorities aside in order to make yourself available. Give any job you receive your full attention and take it efficiently to completion.

- The very first job I received was a huge document sent to me by an agency I had just applied to. The project was to translate a training course for a well-known car company, it was 18,000 words long and needed to be completed within a week.

Although apprehensive and feeling slightly out of my depth, I was determined to respond to the challenge, partly because I was keen to prove myself and get a foot on the ladder and partly because I was grateful for the trust the agency had put in me and I was determined not to disappoint. I managed to complete the work on time, but it was an extremely tight schedule. The agency involved became one of my main sources of work for a number of years and I received an even bigger and more challenging job from them a few years later which kept me busy for over a month!

- Make yourself available at times when other translators are unable or unwilling to take on work, either because they have personal commitments or because their existing workload forces them to turn down additional jobs.

- Take on work that has to be done at unsociable hours. Accepting an assignment on Friday afternoon for a Monday morning deadline means that you will have to work over the weekend, but if this gets you a job, be prepared to do it, at least for a while.

- Work during school holidays or popular public holidays. This will enable you to show your willingness to any agency or business who hires you. If you do a good job, you will have earned some credibility.

- Take on boring jobs! Often you will be offered jobs that are not particularly interesting but again, this type of work is a backdoor to building up your portfolio. This is an essential phase for a lot of newcomers. As soon as you have a regular income, you will be tempted to turn these jobs down yourself, a sure sign that you are on your way and progressing your career.

These are ways of getting started and establishing yourself. Once you have proved yourself a few times with an agency, you are more likely to be contacted again and start receiving more regular work from them.

TOP TIP

Even if you have relatively little or no experience, you can give yourself an edge by being flexible, accommodating urgent requests and taking on jobs that other translators might not be so keen on. This is one way of building up experience and raising your profile.

2. Directories

You can search for directories of translation agencies and companies online and then approach each member one by one. One such directory is the ATC (Association of Translation Companies (www.atc.org.uk). Try and be as personal and approachable as you can. Be prepared to send many applications and to have a low return on your efforts. Don't be despondent as this is one of those compulsory steps that will help you move in the right direction. Don't concentrate on the lack of response, remember that this is typically very low for everybody who goes through the exercise. You must be prepared to sift through many contacts to get to the ones that will work for you. What matters are those first active contacts that you manage to find. When I first started, a friend of mine e-mailed me such a directory with over 100 agencies in it. I ploughed my way through the whole document, which was partly out of date with a number of contacts no longer available. Cold calling was an exercise I didn't enjoy but as a result, I was taken on by three agencies, which gave me regular work for several months, one of them for several years.

3. Membership-based websites

Membership-based websites such as Proz or TranslatorsCafé are useful to raise your profile and gain some experience. You can become a member and post your CV which can be seen by anyone looking for a translator. You can also check job offers for your language pair and bid for jobs which are of interest to you. As an example, one of the most recognised sites is Proz. As well as publishing job offers, it has what is called a 'Blue Board' where you can check whether a particular agency has a good reputation or not. The way it works is that when translators do a job for an agency, they indicate through a rating system whether they are likely to work for that particular agency again or not. This is valuable information as you don't want to risk working for an agency which ends up not paying you. In order to access the Blue Board, however, you need to opt for a partial fee paying membership which costs around £50 per year. You might decide that it is worth paying the fee just for that option and in some cases the membership can pay for itself very quickly. This level of membership also gives you access to job offers which are not available to members who opt for a free membership. The Blue Board enables you to be selective in your choice of agencies by putting them through the Blue Board test before you contact them.

If you choose a free membership with Proz, you can still access most of the other benefits on offer such as chat forums, good terminology databases, an invoicing tool and significant group discounts on the price of translation software packages. Another benefit is that members help each other out with terminology problems. If you answer a query and your answer is selected as the most helpful, you are credited with 'Kudoz points' and this can further raise your profile with potential clients by showing your area of expertise in a particular field. You can also set up alerts for jobs matching your credentials and even set a filter to ensure you only receive notifications for jobs that at least match your minimum rate. Another option Proz offers is the sample translation facility on your profile. You can upload a source and target text which will be displayed side by side. This is something you can mention to potential clients and direct them to the site if they wish to review a sample translation. Other membership-based sites offer similar functionalities.

It is important not to view these membership-based websites as just a direct source of work. A lot of translators do not bid for jobs as the work ends up going to the lowest offer, which can be rock bottom. You should view them more as a marketing tool to find job providers and be found. They can be a very useful shop window and if you view it that way, you won't have the wrong expectations. A lot of companies who use membership-based sites don't necessarily post jobs. They bypass the bidding process and contact directly the translators with the right profile. Such companies are normally happy to pay a decent rate because they value a good translation and quality is important to them.

TOP TIP

You should view your job search as a marketing exercise aimed at raising your profile and being as visible as possible as well as finding work. This will enable potential clients to find you and contact you on their own initiative.

4. Networking

Forums and membership-based websites are more than just a source of direct work, they can lead to jobs through recommendations. Very often, translators post jobs online to other translators, either because they are too busy or because one of their clients is looking for a translator with a different language pair. I have received several jobs that way and have occasionally been able to put a client and a fellow translator in touch. It is always rewarding being able to tell a customer that you have a network of translators whom you trust and can recommend for a job you can't take on yourself. It is a way of extending the service you offer to your client. It is also satisfying to be part of a group where you support each other by passing jobs on whenever possible.

An easy thing you can do is set up an email signature so colleagues and everyone you come into contact with can see your languages, specialisms and contact information. Don't forget to add your website address if you have one. This helps remind people of your skills, even if they are not connected to languages. A friend of mine put me in touch with a lady from her church group who knew someone in Holland who was looking for a translator. This led to a job that kept me busy for a couple of weeks!

5. Your local chamber of commerce

Another initiative you can take is to join your local chamber of commerce. It might not necessarily lead to work straightaway but you might find it useful in many ways. Membership will give you the opportunity to network through various events and get to know professionals in your area. As an organisation, the Chamber of Commerce enjoys a good reputation and many people have positive perceptions of its members and their businesses.

In fact, according to a recent study conducted by the Schapiro Group, 49% of consumers were more likely to think favourably of a local business which is a member of the local Chamber – and 80% were more likely to purchase a product or service from one of its members. Consider membership a long term initiative. It is great for visibility, networking, and community involvement and ultimately, of course, leads. In addition you will have opportunities to socialise, which can energise you, stimulate new ideas and stop you feeling isolated as discussed in Chapter 3.

6. In-house translation departments and direct clients

I believe it is increasingly difficult to find work as an in-house translator as there is a trend amongst companies to outsource translation work to agencies. I never sought to apply for such a position as I wanted to remain freelance, but from experience, it is difficult to find work by contacting companies directly unless you have personal contacts and in-depth knowledge of a specialist area. I remember sending many applications to export businesses and never receiving a single reply. Businesses are working under constant pressure and are inundated with direct mail messages every day from potential suppliers offering a wide range of services. Unless they happen to need your services just as they receive your application and don't know anyone else, your details will not be kept or acted on. I felt at the time that it was an expensive and time consuming exercise and therefore I chose not to continue to pursue that avenue, but that's just my personal experience.

7. Your own website

Websites are quick, easy and cheap to set up. Having your own website might not give you a great advantage in itself, but not having one could put you at a disadvantage because of a growing expectation that everyone nowadays should have an Internet presence. Your website doesn't need to be long or complicated. Just create a few pages to introduce yourself, your specialisms, your experience and anything relevant that will inspire confidence with a prospective client. A few years ago, I was contacted directly by the head of a medium sized manufacturing company based within 20 miles from where I live who had found me via a search online for local translation services. They provided me with work for about 18 months, translating all their marketing literature. I wasn't aware of that company before being contacted by them and being found that way reinforced my opinion that having a website is invaluable.

8. Tradeshows

Tradeshows are great for gathering valuable information and making new contacts. They enable you to raise your profile and find new business opportunities through face to face conversation with potential clients. One example is The Language Show which takes place in London every year. It offers many free workshops on topics that are of direct interest to translators such as what agencies are looking for, how to market yourself or how to brush up on your skills. It is definitely worth attending, and even the more experienced translators find it valuable and stimulating as it is easy to fall into a routine and stagnate.

9. Personal contacts from previous jobs

If you have had a previous career and have been a professional in a given field for a number of years, you might find that you have a client base waiting for you. Just make sure that you inform your colleagues and work contacts about your newly chosen career and they will be pleased to send work your way if they have any need for translation services. People have a natural tendency to use people they know and like, and if you have a proven track record in a specific discipline, you will find yourself busy soon after starting.

10. Listing in a local directory

My experience from putting an advertisement in local directories is that they don't really work. You are far more likely to be contacted by people who use local directories to sell their services and as a result you might get a lot of cold calls from companies trying to sell you advertisement space, office equipment or training programmes. The most likely people to contact you for work from an ad in a local directory are private individuals with small jobs such as translating a private letter, dealing with an invoice relating to a property abroad or making phone calls on their behalf. Sometimes, private individuals have no notion of what the translation process involves or what the cost is and you might find yourself having to educate them on the basics around your work. Personally I found these requests less rewarding. I prefer to deal with companies, but some translators might enjoy these types of jobs and the personal interactions that come with it.

11. Voluntary work

If you are an absolute beginner and you are struggling to find your first job, you will sometimes be advised to do some voluntary work, mainly for charities. For example Translators without Borders is a non-profit association set up to provide pro bono translation services for humanitarian non-profits. You have to know, however, that this kind of work rarely leads directly to paid work. However, it can be valuable as a way to gather experience to put on your CV. If you work for a high profile charity and the document you are translating is going to be published, you can ask for your name to appear on the publication. It's a small attempt at getting noticed that can pay off. A few years ago, I was offered work from a charity through a personal contact. This small charity needed to translate a series of fun brochures targeted at young children in West African countries with the aim to teach them how to protect endangered species in their environment and grow more food cheaply. Although the charity actually paid me, it was half my usual rate and to 'make up' for the low rate, they offered to print my name on their literature. Although it hasn't led to anything else so far, I found the job hugely fulfilling and I was pleased I could take it on at a time when I wasn't particularly busy. I was also more than willing to reduce my rate for a very worthy cause.

CONCLUSION

There are various sources of work you can explore and it is a good idea to try out different avenues simultaneously to give yourself the best chances to find work without having to wait too long. It can be a lonely time and feel like hard work when you get started. Try and attend events aimed at translators like seminars and training days, join forums where you get the chance to speak to others in the profession and share. It is always useful to exchange notes on your experience of job hunting and tips on what works and what doesn't. This also gives you moral support as you realise that everyone is in the same boat when they start.

In order to be a successful freelance translator, you will also need to hone skills that are not about your language capabilities and I will explore these in the next chapter.

Chapter 5

DEVELOPING NON-LANGUAGE BASED SKILLS

Fluency in at least two languages and having a high level of writing skills with perfect grammar and spelling in your mother tongue are, of course, prerequisites to being a translator.

However, in order to be a successful translator you need to possess other qualities which are not language related. Developing these will help you establish yourself more quickly and ensure you free up the maximum time for paid translation work.

Skill 1: Develop good client communication skills

- **When you receive an enquiry**

  When potential clients call you or e-mail you about a possible job, you need to convince them that you are credible and trustworthy, so it is worth spending some time anticipating such a conversation. When you receive a request, sound knowledgeable by answering questions with the assurance of an experienced translator.

  Ask some basic questions about the subject matter, the length of the job, the urgency, the format required, in order to assess whether you can accept the work or not – again this makes you sound prepared and professional. When asked, be prepared to state your rate, but always ask to see the text before committing in case of unexpected difficulties that might slow you down and jeopardise the agreed deadline. Remember also to ask for a purchase order number or a confirmation by e-mail that you have been given the go ahead. Finally, ensure that you agree on payment terms to make sure your interaction is as smooth as possible and paves the way for a possible long term relationship (see Chapter 7 for more).

- **When clients need to be aware of some aspects of your work**

  Many people view translation as a simple exercise of replacing a word by another one in a different language and are unaware of the challenges posed. They don't know that the work requires a creative mind, resourcefulness and imagination. Sometimes it helps to make the client aware of the work involved if it influences the delivery time or the quality of the end result. Your clients will appreciate your efforts more if you explain what is involved and why a good translation cannot be rushed.

- **When you negotiate rates**

  Be aware what rates you can charge according to the nature and degree of difficulty of the text to be translated, your experience, language pair, specialism and what other translators might charge for similar jobs. You can find information about rates that are relevant to you by talking to other translators, and through discussion in forums. Overall, the way you answer questions about rates must reassure the client that you have thought things through and you can be trusted.

  It is also a good idea to have a minimum charge for small jobs. When a client asks you to translate just a title or a short paragraph, explain that you have a minimum rate for small jobs, otherwise you will be working for very small amounts which are not worth your while by the time you have done the job and invoiced for it. Plus, this is not the way you want to be working and any decent agency or company will understand that.

- **When you negotiate deadlines**

  One of the first things you will want to assess about a new translation assignment is how long it will take you to complete. Always ask to see the document before confirming a delivery date as this enables you to properly assess the length of time required for the job. Find out from the client by when they need the translation and check if this is feasible for you, taking account of the length and difficulty of the text, your knowledge of the subject matter and how busy you are. If there is a risk that you might not be able to finish it, say so as soon as possible. If you would like a bit more time, ask if there is any leeway and explain that a slightly longer deadline gives you the time to do a better job. If the client is relaxed about the deadline, you can set yourself one and confirm when they can expect to receive your work. Having a date to focus on will make you work more efficiently. I sometimes find that if I have too much time to complete a job, I tend to lose my concentration and dwell on the job probably longer than I need to.

- **When there are potential problems with the text**

  When you start a job, the golden rule is to raise any queries about the text – whether you have a problem with a specific word, the format, etc. – as soon as possible. Reacting quickly makes you look sharp and efficient and you avoid delaying the delivery of the job. Remember, however, to complete an initial draft first so that you can group all your questions and contact your client only once in order to take up as little of their time as possible. Never use late queries to try to extend a deadline. Contacting the client early will strengthen your credibility. You should bear in mind that when you go back to the client with a query, they might also need some time to revert to a colleague to find the answer, especially around technical terms.

- **When you respond to a query or a complaint**

  Some clients react strongly when they think they have spotted a mistake. Should this happen, your aim is to diffuse the situation regardless of where the problem comes from. Remember that no one is immune to making a mistake, and recognising this as a possibility will help you look at the problem in a more open and detached way. If the fault lies with you, acknowledge it and apologise, saying that you will do everything in your power to make sure this doesn't happen again. When it turns out that the client misinterpreted what you wrote, remain courteous and state that you are pleased the query has been resolved satisfactorily.

TOP TIP

Good communication skills are essential. They will enable you to demonstrate that you are professional, educate your clients when necessary and smooth out any potentially sensitive situation.

Skill 2: Be disciplined and organised

One of the bigger problems of working from home is the temptation to be distracted by your surroundings and engage in so-called "displacement activity". To give yourself the best chances of sticking to your schedule, there are several things you can do:

- **Write a plan in bullet points the day before and stick to it**

  When you have a lot of work and you want to use your time as efficiently as possible, it is advisable to write a plan the day before. It will focus your mind on the important things and is a more efficient method than drawing up a quick list in the morning. Because you have thought about the work in advance and planned it, you are more likely to achieve it. Writing things down makes it more 'official' and you don't want to be disappointed with yourself by failing to stick to your schedule.

- **Take your laptop and work somewhere else**

  You can for example go to your local library or a quiet coffee shop where you can use the free Wi-Fi to work. This can feel more like being in an office environment; it removes all the distractions from home and you just get on with what you need to do. Set yourself a target or even a challenge on what you want to achieve before you leave home - it will give you a greater incentive to reach your goal for the day.

- **Establish rules with friends and family**

  If you share your home with other people, you will need to ask for their cooperation in respecting your work space and avoiding distractions at specific times. If you have older children, part of the plan could be to let them do more for themselves in order to free up as much time for your work as possible.

- **Don't ignore the small details around you**

- Declutter the room where you are working. You will concentrate better, put more energy into your work and you are less likely to interrupt what you are doing.

- Give yourself sufficient space to lay out your drafts and correct your work on paper.

- Ensure you have good lighting for maximum concentration.

- Avoid sources of noise.

- Concentrate on one client and one job at a time and give yourself sufficient time to finish a job before moving on to the next one by negotiating deadlines.

- **Avoid distraction**

  In his book 'Happiness by Design', Professor Paul Dolan shows what a huge cost distraction can have. He explains that distraction is very different from taking a break and that it comes from internal disruption such as intrusive thoughts and from external stimuli such as people and e-mails. Taking a break, on the other hand, he says, is a deliberate and controlled action which can increase creativity. He goes on to explain that distraction is damaging because it requires *switching costs* in terms of energy needed to change from one task to the next. The brain has to reorient itself and if you do this frequently, your attention reserves quickly diminish, making it harder to focus. This is why you have to be wary of modern technology and ensure that using it doesn't eat away at your time. Professor Dolan further explains that in that sense multitasking is not an effective way of working and reduces productivity.

I think this is an important point to emphasise. Personally it has made me more aware of the danger of getting distracted and as a result, I can say that I work more efficiently. Based on this fact, I would suggest that you reduce distraction to a minimum by taking some steps such as:

- Have everything you need within reach (dictionaries, files, external disk drives, etc.) and have your files on your computer organised so you don't lose concentration looking for something or rearranging things.

- Turn off your e-mail account and only check messages at spaced intervals. There isn't much even in this day and age that cannot wait for a couple of hours for your attention.

- Make a conscious decision not to deal with any personal paperwork or household chores and stick to it. Remind yourself that if you were working in an office, you wouldn't be able to do any of these things anyway.

- Manage/educate your family, house sharers, etc. so they understand that you cannot be disturbed any more than if you were working outside in an office.

TOP TIP

Reduce distraction to a minimum and take controlled breaks. Switch your e-mail account off, manage those around you and maximise your working time.

Skill 3: Have flair, creativity and imagination.

Translation isn't just about putting words or ideas in a different language. This might be a rough description of the process itself, but translating requires a lot of flair, creativity and imagination. To achieve this, you need to take account of many different factors: the author, the purpose of the message, the audience, possibly the wider context, and the appropriate tone of the message. An internal memo won't be drafted in the same way as an announcement targeted at international clients or shareholders. Translating a leaflet on a London theatre show will give you a lot of freedom to describe a particular performance and make it appealing to a prospective audience, whereas a contractual agreement will require you to adhere very closely to the original text. You need a keen sense of the best way to express a thought or idea in order to communicate well and have the desired effect.

- Dig into your personal resources and experience, your reading, check what a word or phrase sounds like when you write it down and ensure that it fits. Keep a critical mind and check every detail.

- Keep feeding your mind, be curious and open. Anything you hear or read can be valuable material for your work. I frequently make a note of new phrases or words I come across on the radio. I usually recognise the exact equivalent in my source language but often I haven't heard them in my target language. Every time you glean a new word or phrase, you feel you are adding to your skills and you feel empowered.

Skill 4: Be a perfectionist

Great attention to detail is extremely important. That means concentrating on the slightest nuances of the language and checking the extent of a meaning in both languages. It also means checking your work several times to avoid mistakes (more about this in Chapter 7).

By the time you are ready to send your translation, you will need to have erased all doubt in your mind about any aspect of the text you were translating.

Being a perfectionist also means systematically adding new words and phrases to your glossary to make your next job quicker, easier and better. Ask to see what changes the client makes to the text and build your own glossary for future reference. This will save you time in the long run, improve the quality of your work and increase your confidence in your skills and abilities.

Skill 5: Develop good work ethics

Your reputation is paramount and this is determined by your attitude towards your work and your clients. Treat your clients with respect and never take them for granted. They will appreciate you for it, you will give yourself the best chances of keeping them for a long time and they might recommend you. They will also be happy to write you a reference should you need one.

- The first thing is to be extremely reliable, and that means delivering what you promised, when you promised. Therefore, always stick to your deadline and your customers will know that they can always count on you. That is why it is important to assess a job realistically when you receive an enquiry and suggest a deadline which you are confident you can meet. It is always better to under promise and over deliver.

You can reinforce your reputation of reliability by being proactive and informing the client on the progress of the job without being prompted, especially if you are working on a large document. Many customers say to me: “I wish everyone would do the same”. You have to imagine how reassuring it is for someone who is possibly overworked and has deadlines of their own to be told all is going well and the work will be sent on time.

- Always inform your customers about your absence when you are travelling or going on holiday, even if you are going to be away for the day. That way you will avoid disappointing or irritating them if they send you an urgent request first thing in the morning. Sending a notice of absence serves as a reminder to regular clients that you are still around and they are more likely to remember you as a result and use your services again in future. You can also set up an ‘out of office’ message in your e-mail account.

TOP TIP

For larger projects, you can offer to deliver the work in sections, which enables the client to see how the work is progressing and to start processing it according to their needs.

Skill 6: Adopt a healthy lifestyle

In order to function properly and work at the top of your ability, it helps to adopt a healthy lifestyle. This doesn’t mean leading an austere life, but simply following some simple principles which, incidentally, are also prerequisites for many other careers.

- **Get enough sleep**

  If you are tired, you can still work on a first draft because at that stage you don’t have to be perfect and you will have something to work on when you come back to it more refreshed. But when you are at the stage where you are reviewing your work and performing quality checks, you will want to be as wide awake and concentrated as you can possibly be, drawing on your writing and language abilities, your memory and your imagination. This is why good sleep is important. I know that if I lack sleep, I won't have the same creative ability to write sentences or come up with solutions to challenging words, or ideas for research and the quality of my work will suffer.

- **Work around your natural rhythm**

  Be aware of when you perform best and work around your natural rhythm, whether you are an 'early bird' or an 'owl'. Personally, I like to be up early and get started when I am the only person who is awake in the house. This is when I perform best and I always make the most of that time of day, knowing that my energy level and concentration are likely to drop by early afternoon.

- **Have a physical activity**

  Working from home should enable you the flexibility to escape to a gym or an exercise class, or go for a walk or a run for at least a short session from time to time. I find exercise beneficial as it breaks up the routine of being indoors and doesn't take too much time out of my day. This is also part of why we choose this type of career, for the work-life balance it offers.

- **Have a healthy diet**

  An obvious piece of advice I don't need to go into. Just be aware that working from home can increase the temptation to grab a snack.

CONCLUSION

To be a successful freelance translator requires more than language skills alone. You need to be able to communicate effectively with a wide range of people in different situations, have a professional attitude towards your work and pay attention to practical aspects of your work environment to minimise distractions and promote concentration. Work hard and remember to take regular breaks. The nature of the work enables you to enjoy a satisfactory work-life balance and it is one of the main reasons a lot of people embrace it, so be sure to make the most of it.

You can always improve on all the points listed, regardless how good you think you are at following them. These are life skills which will serve you not only in your translation work but also in other aspects of your life.

In the next chapter, I will be talking in detail about some of the positive and negative aspects of working as a freelance translator.

Chapter 6

PROS AND CONS OF WORKING AS A FREELANCE TRANSLATOR

For many, going freelance is a dream, for others it's something too daunting to contemplate. Whatever your ideas about working for yourself, this chapter aims to evaluate some of the pros and cons of being a freelance translator, which of course are largely the same as for other freelance jobs. Let's look at the advantages first and allow you to get started with a clearer idea of what might be ahead.

Advantages of working as a freelance translator

When you work as a freelance translator, you are working for yourself, most likely as a sole trader and this has numerous benefits:

- **Job satisfaction**

  You have created your own work environment and this alone is exciting: you make all the decisions, you organise your work to best suit you and have a sense of freedom because you don't need to report to anyone – except, of course, to your customers. Your work is stimulating because you have chosen to work with languages, which you are passionate about. You are in the driving seat and this brings a lot of job satisfaction.

- **Pleasant work environment**

  You don't need to worry about office politics or a difficult boss and can produce a great amount of work with fewer interruptions in a pleasant and stress free environment.

  You can work according to your body clock in order to maximise your productivity. Take a short break when it suits best, replenish your energy, and focus on tasks that demand your full concentration when you are at the top of your energy level. When you feel it drop, you can move to routine work such as issuing invoices and other administrative tasks.

Personally I like to get up, make a coffee and get started. I find it particularly energising to work when there is absolute peace and quiet around me. Having made the most of my early morning, I will, of course, tend to flake out a bit by early afternoon and this is where I find a proper break really refreshing before going back to work. Provided you are disciplined and keep these breaks within limits, I think being able to work to your own body clock not only maximises your productivity, but also gives you a great deal of satisfaction.

You are not exposed to age discrimination. This can be a positive factor if you have decided to embrace translation as a career slightly later in life. I have friends who are very conscious that they are surrounded by colleagues ten to fifteen years younger than themselves and although there is no discrimination where they work, they can't help but feel slightly vulnerable. As a freelance translator, you are not exposed to this kind of pressure. Provided you are responsive towards your clients, you maintain your skills and keep abreast of changes in terms of evolving language and technology, age is irrelevant.

- **Flexible hours and locations**

You can organise your time as you wish and decide how much you want to work, whether part time of full time. A lot of people dream of working for themselves and choosing their hours. You don't have the stress of having to take time off for routine appointments, to sort out practical problems or cope with emergencies. (Although you must not allow yourself to be carried away by other activities – more on this in the next section).

You can work from any location, provided you have a laptop and an Internet connection. I have sometimes taken my laptop on holiday when I knew that I was going to have time to do some work. When you work for yourself and you have regular clients who trust you and count on you, you don't want to be unavailable for too long. Provided you don't go to an area with no internet coverage, your clients don't need to know where you are and it saves you having to tell them you are unavailable, so long as you have agreed a suitable deadline.

You are most likely to be working from your own home and that in itself brings valuable advantages:

- **Savings on job related costs**

  You have no commuting time and this represents a great saving not only in time and energy but also in travel costs. You might even save the expense of a car or a second car depending on your situation – worth remembering with all the related expenses of fuel, maintenance, tax and depreciation – when you compare your earnings to other professions.

  You don't have to invest in an extended wardrobe just for your job. Again, this represents a valuable saving. You don't have to sacrifice part of your income to renew business suits and refresh your wardrobe and you have more to spend on smart casual outfits instead!

  Being a freelance translator is a career choice with a low entry cost. You don't need a large capital investment to get started and you might already have some of the equipment you will need, which reduces the entry level cost even further (refer to Chapter 8 for more details on how to set yourself up). If you are leaving paid employment to start working as a freelance translator, you will need to have some money set aside to support yourself at the beginning as you won't have the necessary volume of work to maintain your income level. Alternatively, it may be possible to start translating part-time or work in the evening while staying in your current job.

- **Quality of life**

  To a certain extent, you can choose the type of work you do once you have specialised in an area and built up a large enough customer base to be able to select the work that appeals to you most. For example, I am personally not keen on translating CVs, which have few words but can be tricky and therefore time consuming. When I receive an enquiry to translate a CV or a birth or marriage certificate, I offer to put the requester in touch with another translator who specialises in that type of work and who will be pleased to take on the job. As mentioned in Chapter 3, this is part of being in a community of translators. Helping a prospective client as well as passing on some work to a fellow translator adds to your job satisfaction.

- **Good work-life balance**

  You can achieve a good work-life balance – this is one of the biggest advantages of working for yourself as a freelance translator. Of course some translation assignments are demanding with tight deadlines, challenging texts and sometimes home cooked meals have to be replaced by ready-made options. But generally, working as a translator offers a fulfilling work-life balance with quality time, which means that weekends are not spent catching up on chores or preparing for the week ahead.

  If you have young children, you can organise your work around them while enjoying seeing more of them than you would in another job. Even if you need to organise childcare on a part time basis you are still saving money and you have the luxury of being at home while earning an income. I believe being around as a parent is greatly beneficial for children. You can take them to activities, which childminders are often unable or unwilling to do. Provided the venue lends itself to it, you can even work where the activity takes place.

> If you have made the decision to stay at home to look after your children, it is still important for them to see you work. That way they will perceive you as more than a stay at home parent dedicated entirely to them. They will understand that you have a life of your own and they will learn to respect and accept that some of your time is for other things and other people. When they are old enough to understand, they will know that you are a working professional and you contribute to the family's wealth. Personally, I think this is an important consideration.

When you move from employed work to freelance work, you need to be clear what you are leaving behind and what you are embracing. You might have to give up some benefits, but you are opting for a different lifestyle which might better suit your personality and situation. Although you will have to be more self-sufficient and have the discipline and willpower to make a success of this new career, it can be an exciting challenge. You will need to reach out to other people and that in itself can be the start of a new set of skills you will enjoy developing. You will have the opportunity to experience a different working environment with more freedom, less pressure and greater job satisfaction than a job as a paid employee.

Disadvantages of working as a freelance translator

Every job has its drawbacks and this is no different for freelance translators. The following points are aspects to take into consideration in order to make a fully informed decision before you launch yourself into this career. Some of these aspects might not necessarily be a problem for you, others can be managed or are outweighed by the benefits inherent to the job. It is therefore important not to lose sight of the main reasons why you want to become a freelance translator and go into it with your eyes open. You can use the following list to find out whether you are sufficiently motivated to work for yourself and passionate enough to work as a freelance translator.

- **You are responsible for everything**

  With the thrill of being in the driving seat comes the responsibility of having to manage all aspects of the job, not just translation related work. Therefore some of your time will be taken up by activities that are unrelated to languages:

  + **Marketing and client communication**

    You will need to undertake a certain amount of marketing to generate work and keep increasing your client base and sources of income, especially at the beginning of your career. Even when you are established, it is a good idea to keep in regular touch with clients to remind them that you are still around and available for work should they need your services

  + **Administrative work**

    No one enjoys those tasks but they have to be done and kept under control. Whether it is issuing invoices, sorting out and filing receipts for tax purposes, working out how much money to set aside for tax, tracking outstanding payments or sending reminders to late payers, it all has to be dealt with and can't be delegated. Obviously these tasks encroach on the time you have available to do paid work so be aware and keep on top of them by being organised.

  + **Maintaining your skills**

    You will need to keep up with evolving language and terminology from the industries, sectors or specialisms and affairs relating to your areas of expertise. You will have to take time out to brush up on your skills and maintain them. This will involve reading, learning, going on courses, sometimes making tough decisions on whether a particular course is worth attending, considering the cost, time away from your desk and additional expenses such as travel.

All these activities take time for which you don't get paid, but you should see them as actions and measures aimed at maintaining and increasing your existing income. To a certain extent, the way you see these is down to your personal outlook. You might thrive under pressure, take pride in a job which you have created for yourself and enjoy looking after every aspect as the rightful owner of your business! Furthermore, when you fund a training course or programme yourself, you tend to select more carefully. For that reason, it feels more valuable as this is something you are granting yourself and you are highly motivated when it comes to putting what you have learnt into action.

- **You don't have the benefits of being part of a team**

  If you were previously working as an employee, you might miss certain aspects of your former job which come from being part of a team: a clearly defined role, shared responsibilities, access to help on aspects you are less familiar with and social interaction. When you have a boss to report to, it is easier to keep your concentration and your motivation as you usually have targets to achieve within a given time, so you are less likely to procrastinate. Your colleagues can be a source of moral support and important social contacts which keep you interested and stimulated, possibly through healthy competition and the desire for promotion. You are more likely to keep abreast of changing trends in your field of work and up to date through training at work or outside of work because it is expected as part of your role. As a freelance translator, you haven't got all that support around you.

- **You don't have the financial benefits paid employment offers**

  When you are self-employed, you don't have access to the financial benefits employees enjoy such as paid holidays, sick leave or pension provisions and, as mentioned above, you have to fund your own training. What's more, work can fluctuate and this has an immediate effect on your income. When you take on a large volume of work, you have the stress of dealing with deadlines and when the work is scarce, your revenue takes a dip.

- **There is no clear limit between your work life and your private life**

One of the drawbacks of working for yourself is that your professional and private life can become blurred, especially if you live and work in the same place. On one hand it can be hard not to be distracted by your surroundings when you try to concentrate on your work and on the other hand you cannot physically walk away from your job with your desk and your computer being constant reminders of it. Your working life can therefore encroach on your free time, especially if you have a large volume of work and tight deadlines. Because you can be contacted with new requests at any time, it is hard to switch off or turn them down, and you might find yourself working longer than you would in paid employment and outside normal office hours.

You can control this situation to a certain extent by being fully aware of this danger and by consciously setting some limits. Learn to evaluate realistically how long a job will take you, try and negotiate longer deadlines, aim to finish your first draft quickly and later on your whole translation within the limits you have set yourself. Also make a habit of closing down your PC at a time you set in advance and stick to it.

CONCLUSION

All jobs come with advantages and disadvantages and by considering the aspects described in this chapter you will be far better informed and able to make clear decisions about your future direction.

When you opt to work as a freelance translator, you choose a career path which gives you freedom to organise your life according to your personal priorities and situation. You work in a safe, peaceful environment, the work is interesting, stimulating and keeps you on your toes. On the other hand, you are responsible for all aspects of your work and income. You have to create your own momentum and you won't have the benefits that come with paid employment.

Some of these points won't apply to you or won't affect you greatly and you might consider some aspects, such as being responsible for everything, positively rather than negatively. Overall, as with any new venture, go in with your eyes open and be informed as possible (e.g. by reading a book like this one!)

In the next chapter, I will take you through the translation process in detail and explain what else needs to happen, once you have sent a translation in order for your assignment to be complete.

Chapter 7

THE TRANSLATION PROCESS AND WHAT THE WORK ENTAILS

The aim of this chapter is to give you concrete information about the actual work of a translator on a day to day basis. From responding to an enquiry from a potential client to working on a draft and researching specific terms, delivering the work and ensuring good 'after care' service, the translation process involves several clear stages which have to be followed properly. This chapter will give you a clear idea of what it feels like to work as a translator.

1. Getting a new translation request

Let's just assume that you receive an enquiry from a prospective client. If it is a telephone enquiry you can confirm a few basic details such as your availability, language pair and speciality subjects in order to establish the relevance of the caller's request and whether you can be of service to them. If that is the case, you should ask a few questions in order to determine whether you can take on the job. You will need to ask about the following:

- **Nature of the document**

  Is it an official document such as a marriage or birth certificate, a contract, a press article, an advert? There will be some types of document which you will be familiar with and happy to work on and others you won't. By asking questions about the document you will quickly find out whether this is a job you want to accept or not.

- **Subject matter**

  You do not necessarily have to be familiar with the subject matter. With the nature and extent of help available to translators nowadays, it is possible to carry out some good research quickly on a subject that is new to you, provided it isn't exceedingly technical. You need to ensure, however, that you can do a good job and therefore it is advisable to ask to see the document in order to evaluate the content, level of difficulty and subject matter before committing yourself.

- **Purpose of the document**

  Is the text for publication, or for information only for understanding or professional communication? If the customer is a company, is it an internal or an external document? Knowing this will help you establish the tone and get the right choice of words to fit the intended audience.

- **Length of the document**

  It is important to estimate the length of time you will need to complete the job and assess whether you can fit it into your schedule, depending on work you already have and how quickly the client needs the translation. Obviously the length of a text isn't the only factor to determine the time required to complete, but knowing the wordcount enables you to give your client a good indication. It is accepted, as a general rule, that a translator can do about 2,000 words a day. The work can, of course, take more or less time depending on your experience, the subject matter, etc. But this is a good base to start from when you speak to a client. If you have limited experience and you want to play it safe, work out your delivery times based on 1500 words a day. This will enable you to find out how comfortable you are with that volume of work and adjust accordingly in future. The bottom line is not to put yourself under too much pressure and not to risk missing your deadline.

TOP TIP

If you work in Word, you will be able to see the word count displayed at the bottom of the document. For PowerPoint, select File/Information/Properties/Advanced Properties/Statistics. For other formats including images and PDFs, there are tools such as Abbyy FineReader which can convert documents into editable formats and give you a word count.

- **Format of the document**

  Is the client happy for you to work in a widespread format such as the Microsoft Office package or is delivery required in a format which you are not familiar with or do not have the software for? Does the client expect the delivered translation to be in the same format as the original document? You need to double-check this before accepting the job.

  Another aspect to consider is that the translated text is often a different length to the original. If the text you are translating refers to page numbers, these might end up being different in your translation and you must allow additional time to check page references and pagination and draw the customer's attention to this.

- **Deadline for the job**

  Try to deliver quickly but don't get yourself into trouble by overpromising. It is a good idea to give yourself some leeway in case the job is more challenging than you first thought or you get delayed unexpectedly. It is important to manage the client's expectations, especially if this is a new client and you want to make a good impression and hopefully have them become a regular customer.

TOP TIP

Get the answers to the above points before you start

Try to have all these aspects dealt with so that there are no surprises left either for you or the client. This doesn't take a lot of time and will enable you to establish a clear picture of the task ahead. That way, if you come across some unexpected difficulty, you will be in a much better position to discuss it, as you will have given an impression upfront of someone who is reliable, professional and experienced.

How much to quote – time and money

Very often, when you receive an enquiry by phone the first question a potential client will ask is: 'How much does the translation cost?'. Explain that your price depends on the length of the document and the difficulty of the text. You can give a price range (usually per 1,000 words) but always stress that this is just an indication and you will confirm the definite price once you have had a chance to look at the text and assess it properly. If the client isn't familiar with the translation process, he or she might need some background information on the way you work. It is a good idea to know how long a text will take so you can indicate an approximate number of hours needed to complete the job and a delivery time. This might help the client see the real value in your work by realising that a good translation needs time to complete.

Let them know that you might have queries on the text. If it is a long document or an urgent assignment, you can tell them that you will keep them informed of your progress and that you might revert to them with questions.

Over time, you will get accustomed to quoting your rate and you will have a feel for whether you are being paid a fair price for your work or not. You have to take your time into account, but also the standard of living it gives you and what others are charging. If you think you are charging too little, increase your price at the next enquiry. Remember not to compete on price as there will always be someone somewhere who is charging a lower rate than you, so don't be caught up in that spiral. Your focus should be to offer value through your skills, your attitude and your professionalism. I would even argue that charging a decent price is somewhat reassuring for some clients. A lot of companies are ready to pay for a service they can trust. They understand that they get what they pay for and that a cheap translation might end up costing them a lot more through rework, wasted time and, worst of all, misunderstanding or a damaged reputation.

TOP TIP

Communication is key: it doesn't have to take long, but a short message reporting on progress is reassuring, especially for a new customer who has decided to put their trust in you but doesn't know yet that you are going to deliver on your promises.

Accepting the work

Always ask to see the work first before you commit. There may still be occasions where a document isn't available in electronic format, in which case you will need to receive a fax or a scanned copy). Ask your client to e-mail you the document so you can assess it and decide whether this is something you can do and how long it will take. Once you have decided to accept, send the client a short quote in writing, confirming all the details regarding delivery time and price agreed. Confirm that you are pleased to accept the job and ask the client to send you a purchase order number. If they don't issue purchase order numbers, the very least you should insist on is a confirmation in writing that they are giving you the go ahead. This can simply take the form of a short e-mail asking you to start immediately.

TOP TIP

Always ask to see the document before you firmly commit.

You can give your agreement in principle, but always subject to seeing the full document. Only then can you estimate accurately how long it will take and have the assurance that this is a job you can tackle.

2. Taking on a new client

When a project comes from a new client, you don't know that person or organisation and you might ask yourself whether they are trustworthy and reliable before accepting work from them. The following are considerations you can take into account:

A fine balance

Ideally you want to set clear rules which define each party's rights and responsibilities. On the other hand, you want to make it as quick and easy as possible for a potential client to deal with you and remove anything that might be perceived as unnecessarily formal, cumbersome and time consuming. If you are dealing with direct clients, you can present your terms and conditions and get the client to sign a contract if you feel that it gives you better protection. Personally, I have always gone down the informal route and my experience with all new customers has always been a positive one.

If you work through agencies, you will find generally that they have their own terms and conditions to which they ask you to adhere. Read these carefully before signing anything as terms can vary widely between agencies and some will have clauses which you might find excessive or unacceptable. This topic is often discussed on translators' forums.

My own experience is that you can trust your intuition and pick up a lot from just talking to people. Once you have concluded your initial conversation with a prospective client, you can look them up online to find more details about who they are. As mentioned previously, if working for an agency, you can try and find out whether they have a good reputation by asking around other translators on forums, or checking the Blue board on Proz.com if you are a paying member. Of course there is always an element of risk when you decide to work for someone new, but this is the only way you are ever going to start or expand your business. In the vast majority of cases, your experience will be a happy one.

Non-disclosure Agreements (NDA)

Some companies will ask you to sign a NDA. This is often a routine part of working with a new supplier and the aim of the agreement is as the name suggests, to ensure that the content of any document or information provided to you in the course of working with the company is treated as confidential and not shared or disclosed to any other party. It is quite usual, especially for large companies, to ask you to sign one of these before you start translation work and adhere to the conditions.

Contractual Terms and Conditions

Unless you agree otherwise, you will normally be subject to standard conditions for delivery of services and payment of the company you are working with. These can vary widely, with some larger companies only paying 45 or even 60 days after receipt of invoice. For larger documents, you may be able to agree staged payments. The principle here is to be aware of the terms and conditions and negotiate the best available.

Currency

You may well find that you win work from agencies or companies in other countries. This means you will need to be clear about the currency in which you will invoice and be paid. This is usually very straightforward, but be aware of fluctuating conversion rates which can work for or against you. Also, check with your bank whether a charge applies for receiving money from overseas and whether this is a flat fee or a percentage. For example it might be advantageous to group several jobs on one invoice to receive a single payment and therefore avoid multiple fees.

3. Translating your document

These are the steps I recommend you follow to ensure your translation is of the highest quality:

Step 1: Print your source text

I always find it helpful to have a printout of the source next to me, even when I work with a CAT tool (see Chapter 9) and both languages are displayed side by side on my screen. A paper version also enables me to better visualise the text in context, underline challenging words and write down questions. This makes it easy to draw up a list of queries to go back to the client.

Step 2: Do a first draft on screen

Aim to work quickly through this step and get to the end of your draft before you review it. It is important to keep the momentum. Try to phrase your text as best you can to suit the assignment and don't worry about being perfect at this stage. You can do some basic word searches to keep you moving forward, but keep writing even when you know you will need to change or make improvements later on. Coming back to a text as a separate step immediately raises the quality of your work to the next level.

TOP TIP

Have all your online reference material open and ready to use – such as dictionaries, glossaries and search engines. For example you can have a Google page in your target language, www.studentgems.com or another bilingual dictionary depending on your language pair, Linguee.com and any specialised glossaries that are relevant to your work. You can easily find the right glossary for the subject you are working on by simply typing 'Terminology' followed by the name of your subject into a search engine, whether it is 'marketing', 'milk', 'aviation' or anything else.

Step 3: Check your draft on screen

Check your translation on screen against your source document, either by having the two languages side by side on your screen or by having a printout of your source text next to you. You need to be very focused and check your work against the source text with a critical mind. It is vitally important to be alert and at the top of your ability for this step. In other words, you can't perform this step very well if you are tired or lacking sleep. You must question everything, check the semantic range of each word (i.e. whether the translation has a broader or narrower meaning in one of the languages), the choice of words and the context for the message being conveyed.

Step 4: Group your questions and send them to the client

Once you have completed and checked your draft, group all your questions together and go back to the client with your list. It is important to do this step early, but not before you have checked your draft at least once. This is because you will find some of the answers to your initial questions just by familiarising yourself with the document and having a better understanding of the context. Sending all your questions at this stage means you are still able to progress your translation while you wait for the answers so no time is wasted. By grouping them, you avoid unnecessary communication between you and the client, which is the most effective way of working.

Step 5: Read through your translation on screen

This time, simply read through your work without checking it against the source text. Have a feel for what it sounds like and correct any obvious mistake and anything that doesn't flow or sound right in your target language. This step aims to remove as many errors as possible before you work through the next stage.

Step 6: Print your translation and check both versions on paper side by side

Don't be tempted to skip this step, it would be counter-productive. Regardless how careful you think you are, there will always be mistakes which you simply won't be able to spot on your screen, but which will be obvious on paper straightaway. I sometimes find that a sentence or phrase that might read well on screen doesn't actually sound 100% right when you read it on paper and this is why I consider this a vital step. So never hesitate to print all of your work, even for something that seems short, easy and straightforward.

Step 7: Set the source text aside and concentrate on your translation as if you were editing an original

This will enable you to judge your work almost through the eyes of an outsider and double check all aspects: the spelling and grammar of course, but also the level of language used for the audience and the tone of voice. Does it read like an original? Does it serve the intended purpose (e.g. if it is a piece of advertising or a sales and marketing text, does it sound convincing)? Is it current and elegantly phrased? If at all possible, leave your translation aside for a few hours, or better still, overnight. When you then come back to it, you will see it with fresh eyes and have the necessary distance to review it one more time with a critical mind.

Step 8: Proofreading

Unless your client has the resources to check your translation in house, it is a good idea to team up with another translator who works with the same language pair as you and is familiar with the kinds of subjects you are translating. That way you can proofread each other's translations and discuss possible solutions to tricky or challenging problems. Working as a team gives each of you an additional security and makes your work more fun.

TOP TIP

Use monolingual dictionaries!

One important aspect it took me a long time to appreciate is the importance of monolingual dictionaries. Sometimes, when you read a clear and precise definition of a term, you will notice that the right word in your target language will then spring spontaneously to mind, or it will open a new avenue for additional research.

4. Sending your translation to the client

Once you are happy with your work, send it to the client in the format agreed. Your translation should be accompanied by a short message asking for confirmation that the work has been received.

TOP TIP

Make a habit of systematically checking what you send to your clients. As soon as you have e-mailed your translation, go into your 'Sent' folder and open the file you just sent as it is so easy to click on the wrong file. If this happens, send the correct document with an apology before the client has had time to realise what happened. Also, be available after you have sent your work in case there are problems or queries. This is the kind of attention to detail and attitude that will differentiate you from other translators and your clients will rate you highly for this.

Make mistakes work in your favour!

I was about to start a gym class recently when I quickly glanced at my phone and saw an e-mail from a client telling me that I had sent the original instead of the translation. The work was urgent and the client was asking me to send the right file as quickly as possible. I replied straightaway to reassure them I had received their message and rushed home immediately. Far from being annoyed, the client was grateful! I had shown them that I have their best interest at heart and that they can count on me whatever happens. When you react in this way, you not only gain the client's respect but you stand head and shoulders above your competitors by making yourself indispensable. You are offering top quality service and a reliability that is extremely valuable to other people's work. Therefore when you make a genuine mistake and you correct it as soon as possible, far from damaging your relationship with your client you are actually reinforcing your reputation.

Naming and saving your work

When you start having a number of clients and your workload is increasing, you will need your files kept in a proper order so that you can retrieve them easily. I create a folder for each client and save each file chronologically by starting the name of each file with the date marked as: 'yymmdd Name of file'. For example if I translated a press release on the acquisition of a company called Greenway I would call my file: 160121 Greenway Acquisition.docx. If I work on another file the following day I would call it 160122..... This enables me to retrieve any file easily when I need to refer to something. I save each file twice: in the source language and in my target language as I sometimes need to refer to both languages when I need to look them up.

I have found that this system works for me, but obviously this is not the only one and you might want to organise yourself differently. Whatever method you choose, it's important to decide on a nomenclature structure from the beginning that helps you identify a saved file from its name, even several years after you created it.

5. After you have sent your work

Your job doesn't end when you have pressed the 'Send' button on your computer. There are a few more steps which I recommend you take in order to add more value to your work:

- Ensure that you have sent the correct file.
- Ask the client to confirm receipt
- Ensure you can be contacted by phone or e-mail in case the client needs to get back to you.
- Invite the client to give you feedback.
- Use any feedback you receive to build up your own glossary. This is a chance to learn from every job you do and deepen your expertise in a particular subject. It also enables you to adapt your style to that of the client and minimises the need for corrections in future translations, saves the client precious time and turns you into a valuable resource.

6. Expect changes

In translation, there is no such thing as 100% perfection. No matter how proficient you are and how hard you work, it is likely that there will be some changes to your translation. This doesn't necessarily reflect on the quality of your work and you should expect to deal with changes as an additional step. Usually your translation will be checked by a reviewer who is an expert on the subject matter and the audience for which your translation is intended. The reviewer will then send the document back with changes to be implemented. Only once you have carried out the changes and returned the final version is your translation assignment complete.

7. Archiving

There is just one more step for you to do and that is to archive your document for safety and for future reference. Please refer to Chapter 9 for more details on archiving.

CONCLUSION

Having read this chapter, it might seem to you that translation work involves a lot of steps, but when you actually start you will find that these happen in quick succession and in fact the work feels more like one smooth and straightforward process. By following the structure I have outlined, you will make sure you don't miss anything, keep on track and save time and unnecessary work. Always work with your customers' needs in mind, be accommodating and easy to do business with by getting it right first time. That way not only are you offering good customer service but you are also making your work as easy and efficient as possible for yourself.

In the next chapter, I will explain some key legal requirements you need to have in place, how to prepare applications for work and how to promote your services.

Chapter 8

THE FIRST STEPS: SETTING UP YOUR OWN BUSINESS

In this chapter I will take you through the practical steps needed to set up your freelance translation business. From legal requirements to ways of approaching agencies and writing your CV that get results, follow these stages to get going, compete and reach your goal.

Note: written from a UK perspective. Similar processes will apply in your country of residence.

LEGAL REQUIREMENTS

1) Register as a sole trader

As soon as you start working, you can register as a sole trader. Do this sooner rather than later, as it will encourage you to keep records and you won't risk forgetting to register and be penalised. By being organised from day one, you will get into the habit of keeping important documents safe such as invoices and proof of allowable expenses and this will help you when it comes to filing your tax return. You can register online at https://www.gov.uk/set-up-sole-trader/overview. The website provides information on why you need to register, what your responsibilities are as a sole trader, which rules to observe when naming your business and how to register according to your circumstances. Registration takes 10 working days to be completed and 21 days if you reside outside the UK.

2) Get a national insurance number

If you haven't got a national insurance number, you must ensure that you apply for one. This can be done online at https://www.gov.uk/apply-national-insurance-number with the prerequisite that you are entitled to work in the UK. Similar registration requirements should be completed if you are resident in another country.

APPLYING FOR WORK

Once you have dealt with the legal requirements, you can concentrate on applications for work. This stage requires time and the right amount of preparation, so don't be tempted to rush or overlook any details. You will need to identify potential clients and research them as it is important to carefully adapt your message in each application to increase your chances of receiving a positive response. Above all, set yourself the right expectations and be aware that this phase can take some time.

Write your CV

The first thing you need is a CV. This is the most important tool to get you started and it is vital to compose it with great care. Ideally you should stick to two pages, three at a maximum and only include information relevant to your application as a translator. A good CV will be clear, concise and to the point. Think of it as a sales document to present yourself in the best possible light.

As you are applying for work as a translator, it is a good idea to have a strong section for language skills. Emphasize the degree of proficiency you have achieved and the depth of your experience with languages.

Present every section with a clear title in bold, even in a box if you like. This makes it easy for the reader to absorb the content and navigate quickly between sections. Information given under each section should be presented in bullet points and sufficiently spaced. Once complete, your CV must be neat, make a good first impression and be easy and pleasant to read.

A good CV should contain the following:

- **Your name** at the top of every page

- **Your contact details** including your website if you have one

- **A short description of yourself** – preferably in the third person, about your achievements, plans and vision for the future

- **Your skills** listed in bullet points with real examples of how you have used them. Remember skills and abilities such as networking and communication. If you struggle to fill in this section, ask people around you what you are good at. You will probably be pleasantly surprised, as we tend to ignore or take for granted skills that we have and others value. This section should also contain your CPD (Continuous Professional Development) track record. This is the process of documenting skills, knowledge and experience that you gain both formally and informally as you work. By working on your CPD, you are showing that you are keen to keep your skills up to date and acquire new ones, as well as demonstrating that you are committed to your career and the translation industry (more on this in the last chapter).

- **Your education and qualification** – schools, universities and other institutions you have attended and qualifications gained.

- **Professional memberships** – agencies value professional memberships and these give weight to your application. For example if you are a member of the CIOL or the ITI, don't forget to mention it.

- **Your employment history** starting with the most recent. Include job titles and describe duties and responsibilities for each job listed.

  If you have limited work experience or you graduated recently, focus on your education instead. Describe work you did whilst studying and list any placements and internships. Show your proficiency through your life experience, state your achievements, what you have learnt and skills you have acquired in the process, including dealing with people, the importance of being reliable, sticking to your commitments, meeting deadlines. Give concrete examples where you have shown determination, strength of character, etc. Did you struggle to get where you are? Have you succeeded in spite of the odds? Mention volunteering and charity work.

- **Interests and activities** – this section might not seem essential but it is another chance to stand out by saying something more personal or emphasising a particular expertise you have.

- **References** – this is the last section. You can list contact details on your CV or simply state 'Available upon request'. Ensure you get for permission from anyone you are naming as a referee.

- Finally, numbering the pages makes your CV look polished and shows you are paying attention to every single detail.

TOP TIP

When you send your CV to an agency, make sure it is in PDF format that cannot be edited. This will protect you against scammers. If you send your CV in Word format, it could be more easily stolen and used by someone pretending to be you. The PDF format doesn't guarantee 100% protection but makes you much less vulnerable as it is harder to modify. This piece of advice is not meant to scare you: scammers do exist and you are better off knowing about them so you can better protect yourself. More on that subject in Chapter 11.

Another reason why your CV should be in PDF format is that if the agency opens it in a different Word version than the one you use, it might upset the layout and won't look its best.

Personal profiles

You can use your completed CV as the foundation for any other personal profile you need, whether written or online. Most often, these profiles are required for websites and will be more succinct and possibly less formal in tone. When writing online profiles, be sure to choose the most relevant and interesting information.

Cover letters

Your cover letter should be short and to the point. Agencies receive applications for different types of language-related jobs, not just translation, so it is important to say in the subject line that you are applying for freelance translation work and to state your language pair. This makes it very easy for agencies to read and assess your application.

Once you have finished your CV, you might be tempted to send applications to as many agencies as you can find with a standard cover letter. Please don't! This would be a mistake which would give you poor results and could leave you disappointed and even disheartened. You would wonder what to do next and might feel you have run out of options. Agencies can tell when someone sends out blanket applications and by doing so you diminish your chances of success and undermine the good work you have done on your CV.

You will need to adapt each cover letter you send and decide how formal or informal you want to be. This is why it is important to do some research beforehand on the company or agency you intend to contact, as every organisation has their own culture and this determines how people communicate. Whatever style you decide to adopt, try to convey the fact that you are passionate about your job, friendly, professional and easy to do business with.

TOP TIP

Remember to state your language pair clearly on your CV as well as in your cover letter. This is the first thing an agency will want to know before they consider your application.

Applying for work with translation agencies

Unless you have personal contacts in a particular industry or some in-depth knowledge on a highly specialised subject, it is generally very difficult for individual service providers to get work with corporate clients. You are far more likely to find work through translation agencies and for that reason the advice I am giving in this chapter is based on the assumption that you are applying to agencies.

Again, do your research before you apply. Not all agencies are the same and you need to find out as much as you can about those you intend to approach. Some agencies specialise in certain fields and if these are different from the ones you intend to work in, you would be wasting time and resources targeting them. Try also to find the name of a manager so that you avoid starting your letter with 'Dear Sir or Madam' which sounds impersonal. Even if you don't have a person's name, it is better to address the letter to a job role.

If you don't get feedback from the agencies you applied to, follow up with a phone call. They won't mind and you will pick up some precious information and good advice on how to improve your application. Perhaps you need to emphasise an important point more, pick up a specific skill, or start using a piece of software which will make you more competitive.

Should you do a test translation?

Some agencies and even direct clients occasionally ask translators who apply for work to do a test translation before commissioning a job. There is a debate in the industry about whether you should accept to do these or not, especially if you are a qualified and experienced translator.

If you are starting out and your experience is limited, this can be a chance to prove yourself and overcome hurdles, especially if you have a degree or other qualifications but no specific qualifications as a translator. Here are some points to consider when deciding:

- If an agency asks you to do a test translation, check first what rates they are paying. It they pay below what you find acceptable, there is no point doing a test in the first place.

- A test translation should be done in relation to a specific job which is normally substantial and fairly specialised. Why should anyone ask you to do a test translation on a general or random subject when they don't know when or whether they will have work for you?

- If you agree to do a test, make sure it is reasonably short (300 to 500 words as a guidance). This should be sufficient to assess your competence as a translator. If the test text is any longer, it could just be that the requester is using you for free work and the test is actually a job in disguise.

I have only ever done two test translations in my career. The first one was for the job on marine equipment I talked about in Chapter 2. It was highly technical and I was competing against an engineer who was a specialist in the field but not a qualified translator. I was awarded the job which was 25,000 words.

The second one was shortly after I had qualified as a translator. An agency I applied to had a client who was looking for a new translator for my language pair. I passed the test over ten years ago now and I am still working for this client today. The agency volunteered to pay me half their normal rate for the test (despite the fact that I didn't ask for anything and they were not getting anything for it themselves). I thought that was very fair.

Would I do another test translation now if I was asked to? I would consider it, but only for a specific project or for a client looking for a long term relationship.

PROMOTING YOUR BUSINESS

Have a website

Creating a website isn't very onerous nowadays and having one definitely helps you stand out. You want to be visible and you want to be found, and having a website enables you to present yourself to prospective clients and show what you are offering with a minimum of effort. An added benefit is that writing your website content constitutes a good marketing exercise: it will make you think about what is unique about you, define what your offering is and give you an identity.

Your website doesn't need to be long or complicated either, a few pages stating the essentials is enough. You will need to choose and register a domain name and then create the actual pages. If you feel that you have sufficient skills, create the pages yourself using tools such as WordPress. If you prefer to delegate the task to a professional and focus on the language side instead, it won't cost you much to commission a web designer. However, it is worth learning how to edit your website yourself to avoid paying someone every time you want to change a detail or add some information. Remember also to ask for an invoice as this is an expense you can offset against tax.

Matching stationery

As networking is part of your marketing activities, you will necessarily come into contact with professionals who will ask for your business card. It happened to me several times just in the last few weeks. It is therefore a good idea to have some stationery printed with the same visual as your website – showing consistency will help people remember who you are. Another useful element of stationery to have is a letterhead form. You don't need to have this printed though, just an electronic version which you can use to send attachments or for correspondence. You can also print letter-headed documents at home if you have a good quality colour printer.

Social Media

In addition to having a website as a place of introduction and to promote yourself to potential clients, consider including digital and social media such as LinkedIn and blogs into your marketing strategy. Potential clients might wish to check your legitimacy, credibility and approach, or simply get in touch and ask questions, so ensure that your social media presence reflects your new translation business and is kept up to date.

- **LinkedIn**

You probably already have a LinkedIn profile. The question to ask yourself is: does this profile reflect the business persona you are now establishing in order to win translation work? Your LinkedIn profile is your shop window, a place to showcase your professional brand, your subject matter expertise, your knowledge and your skill set.

Here are a few examples of actions you can take to improve your LinkedIn presence:

- Add a professional looking picture
- Put your personalised URL (automatically created by LinkedIn) in your e-mail signature, on your business card and anywhere else you publish your contact details
- Add interesting content relating to translation

For more information, search online for tips and tricks to create the perfect profile. They are quick and easy to implement and certainly worthwhile.

- **Facebook**

In essence the same principles apply to Facebook as to LinkedIn. Although Facebook is perceived by some people being more suitable for social than professional interaction, some translators have switched to groups set up on Facebook rather than other forums to ask for help and support each other with their work related queries.

- **Blogs**

  Blogs have become increasingly widespread and are a way of reaching out and being more visible. You might think this is not for you if you are only just starting out but it is another avenue you can explore. Focus on telling a personal story with your impressions and what you have learnt, for example from the time you were studying or from a former job. Just be yourself, be open and honest and as long as you are genuine, people will relate to what you want to say and comment on it. Sharing information is a way of gaining people's trust. It is an enriching experience because you open an avenue for others to gain from your contribution but also to contribute themselves. In that sense it can be a win-win situation.

In summary, when it comes to social media channels make sure they are kept up to date and that the image they portray in words and pictures is connected and coherent across all the touchpoints people might use to connect with you.

CONCLUSION

The road to success is a learning process and there aren't any shortcuts: each application must be carefully crafted to have a chance to make the impact that you want. Don't think of this process as hard work but as a chance to learn to make the next one better: send a few applications first and see what happens. You will have new ideas after a while about what you could do better or express differently. You will be honing your marketing skills as you go along.

In the next chapter, I will talk about some important administration which will help your business run smoothly and provide some tips on what equipment to purchase.

Chapter 9

ADMINISTRATION AND TOOLS OF THE TRADE

Keeping on top of administration is critical to the success of your business and your peace of mind. Of course this is not the most exciting aspect of your new career. Following the advice in the next few pages will help you run your business efficiently on a day to day basis and reduce time spent on these routine tasks. I will also discuss what hardware and software you need to get started.

ADMINISTRATION

Issuing your invoice

Before you get your first job, prepare an invoice template so you can send an invoice as soon as you have finished your first translation assignment. You can design your invoice in your own personal style but there are certain compulsory elements which need to be featured:

- The word INVOICE must appear on the document
- An invoice number (unique to every invoice you create)
- The date of the invoice
- Your company name, address and contact details
- The company name and address of the customer you're invoicing
- A clear description of the services you are charging for
- The date the services were provided (supply date)
- A purchase order number, if applicable. Always ask for one every time you start working for someone new as in some companies it is proof that the job and the funds to pay for it have been authorised.

- The amount(s) being charged
- The VAT amount. This probably won't apply to your situation when you start out, in which case you can just write 'NO VAT APPLICABLE' on your document
- The date payment is due

As you are most likely to be a sole trader, ensure your invoice mentions your own name and an address where any legal documents can be delivered to you if you are using a business name.

If you would like some help to get started, go online and download a free invoice template. Working from an existing model, you can then customise it to suit your own needs. If you have a website, your invoice should reflect your visual identity, as another contribution to raising your profile. Alternatively, Proz.com has an invoice creation facility and offers even non-members the opportunity to produce up to 5 invoices for free, an option you might like to try.

Creating a record of your work for invoicing purposes and to track payment

As soon as you have received a few jobs, you will need to keep a record that will show you at a glance the status of each one. This enables you to track your work and makes invoicing and checking payment due dates easier, and you don't risk overlooking a single one. You can create a simple Excel spreadsheet where you list each job in chronological order with the amount, the client's name, the purchase order number, the name of the file and the date of your invoice. This gives you a complete overview of your job status and income and makes it easy to send reminders in case of late payments.

Personally I use a colour coded system to mark the stages of each job. For example the amounts are in green when I am still working on the files and I change them to red as soon as I have sent off the work. Each client's name is in blue as long as I haven't invoiced them and I change it to black once I have sent my invoice. Finally, when I receive a payment, I change the amount in red back to black. This might seem fiddly but it only takes a few seconds to update my file and works for me. There are plenty of ways to keep track of your jobs including setting alerts in your electronic diary. The main thing is to find something that works for you, is 100% efficient and isn't time consuming.

This document also serves as a record to find earlier files in seconds. I used it very recently to retrieve a translation one of my customers asked me about and which I had done over 5 years ago.

Recording tax allowable expenses

First of all, establish which expenses you can offset against tax. As a general rule, allowable expenses are those you incur for the sole purpose of running your professional activity. They will include the following:

- Office costs such as stationery (paper, files, print cartridges, phone bills, computer repairs, etc. even Christmas cards sent to your customers)

- Travel costs, for example if you attend live events for translators

- Financial costs such as professional indemnity insurance, the cost of an accountant and a bookkeeper if you decide to use such services

- The cost of your business premises. Even if you work from home, you can claim a portion of bills such as gas, electricity, telephone and even council tax bills.

- Marketing costs, for example printing business cards, having your website designed and optimised

Consult the tax authorities online to find out in more detail what constitutes an allowable expense.

To claim expenses, you must keep records and fill in a self-assessment tax return. To make it easier for yourself, have a file in which you keep all proofs of expenses such as receipts and invoices and enter the figures in a spreadsheet. Make a habit of recording these expenses on a regular basis and don't leave it too long between sessions. This will simplify your task when it comes to filing your tax return. All you will then need to do is add up the numbers and transfer the figures to your tax form – you won't waste any time trying to remember what expenses you incurred in the last 12 months or looking for receipts to back them up.

Backing up and safekeeping files

A few years ago, I had a virus on my laptop which caused all my files to disappear, including those on the hard disk drive that was plugged into it. I called on a computer expert who fortunately was able to restore my files. Had that not been possible, it would not have been disastrous as I had a second copy of all my files stored away. I would have lost the latest version of the file I was working on but in the scheme of things this would have been minimal. Instead, my only loss was the cost of hiring the computer expert.

If, however, I had not been able to retrieve my documents, I would have lost more than just my files: my invoices and my job records were also stored on the same device. At the time, I had a number of jobs I hadn't invoiced for and it would have been a struggle to trace them all. That experience definitely reinforced my determination to be vigilant. It can be tempting to postpone that small administrative task but this is a small price to pay to stay safe, as the consequences of not doing so are too great to contemplate.

As soon as you start working, it is advisable to decide on a system to keep your documents and your clients' files safe.

Saving your work

When you work on a document, save your work on a regular basis during the process of translation. Think also of backing up your work to a separate device to protect it from the eventuality of your PC being out of action. Whenever I pause for a while, I automatically save my work both onto my laptop and to an external disk drive. When I finish working for the day the two sources of documents are kept separate. This procedure becomes more and more necessary over time as your work accumulates and you build up a large volume of files which you might need to refer to and which you won't want to lose.

Archiving and safekeeping

Archiving is the storage or preservation of information. By archiving documents, you free up space so your computer handles current documents more efficiently. Although this might not be a problem when you get started, it is a good idea to get into the habit of archiving from the beginning so you don't run into problems when your workload starts to build up. There are several methods for archiving documents:

1. Archive documents on your hard disk drive

If you want to keep your past translations on your hard disk drive, you can zip your files to reduce the space they take. Personally I prefer to have them stored on a separate device which I keep safe and separate from my laptop.

2. Move your documents to an external hard disk drive

External hard disk drives now offer an extremely large storage capacity which should last you for years and they have become very affordable. Furthermore, they are portable and easy to keep in a safe place.

3. Back up documents to a CD or DVD

This is another option but is probably less attractive now that external hard disk drives are so widely available.

4. Send documents to the cloud

This solution offers easy access to your files from any computer with automatic back up against the risk of your equipment being out of action. However there are some drawbacks as no system is 100% safe. Some have clauses that limit your privacy or they don't encrypt files when they are transferred, which could lead to security problems. If you choose this option, do your research to find the right provider.

Summary

Technology is evolving fast and some archive systems could become obsolete over time. This is a consideration to keep in mind before you select your preferred method.

There is always a likelihood that you might need to refer to a particular document again, or that the client might come back to you with a query. Whatever method you choose for archiving, ensure you are thorough and that you have your documents stored on more than one device.

Renewal dates

If you decide to take up professional indemnity insurance, you will need to renew your cover every year. Make a note in your diary to shop around so you have some negotiation power when you are approached by your existing insurance company to renew your policy. Some companies keep insuring all the work you have done from the first day you have a policy through them to try to win your loyalty.

Remember also to renew any subscriptions you have such as professional memberships, trade magazines and possibly some licence renewals for software or online dictionaries or glossaries. Having an efficient paper or digital administration system helps keep these tasks to a minimum and lets you concentrate on activities that bring you an income.

Another date for your diary is the deadline by which your tax return must be received to avoid being penalised. As previously mentioned, this is made easy if, throughout the year, you have been diligently recording every allowable expense as you incurred it.

TOOLS OF THE TRADE

The first thing you need is a dedicated space where can spread your documents and work undisturbed. This doesn't need to be a whole room, but it is important that you can leave your documents, files and dictionaries lying around when you take a break or stop working for the day. This enables you to go back to work quickly and keep distractions to a minimum. Wherever you decide to install your office space, make sure you have proper lighting to work.

In terms of equipment:

- **A comfortable desk and chair** – get a chair that supports your back and is positioned correctly in relation to your desk so that when you sit with your elbows and knees at right angles, your screen is at a height which enables you to look straight at it without looking up or down. It is important to perform these checks to avoid discomfort or problems caused by a bad posture in the long run.

- **A computer** – preferably a laptop, which gives you the flexibility to work away from your usual location when you need to. If you already have a computer but share it with other members of your family, consider getting your own and keep it for your sole use to avoid any potential problems. If you decide to buy a laptop, choose one with a large screen (at least 15 inches) as you will be spending a lot of time in front of it, but more importantly being able to display two documents side by side is something you will need to do for every job.

- **A printer** – to help keep the quality of your work to a high level, it is important to print not only your own translations, but also the original documents in your source language. This is because checking your work on paper is a vital step in the translation process and should not be skipped. For this reason, you will need a cost effective, high productivity printer. A few years ago I attended a translators' seminar during which we were advised to get a laser printer as opposed to an inkjet, as this type of printer is more economical due to its large toner cartridge which lasts longer than any ink cartridges. Things might have changed as technology evolves fast, but whichever option you choose, remember you typically only need to print your documents in black and white and monochrome printers are cheaper to buy than colour ones.

- **Lever arch files** - to store your documents. Ideally you should have one file per client and a separate one for invoices. Although your files will be stored on your computer, it is sometimes quicker to do a rapid search by leafing through paper documents rather than looking through electronic copies.

- **Dictionaries** - although there are many free resources online, there is still value in having a few select printed dictionaries, especially if you are working in a highly specialised area. When I started out, I bought a bilingual dictionary on business, commerce and finance and another one of technical and scientific terms. Although this is well over 10 years ago, I still find myself resorting to them, usually when I have hit a dead end and cannot find an answer online. More often than not, I am surprised to find that they do hold the answer I was looking for.

- **External hard disk drives** –to keep your files safe, as discussed earlier in this chapter.

- **A mobile phone** – to keep in touch and respond to enquiries without delay when you are out and about. I recently went to a translator's event in London for the day and received an enquiry. Because I was in touch through my mobile, I didn't feel the need to let my clients know I was away. Instead, I was able to download the document and estimate the time it would take me to do the work. I responded quickly and confirmed that I could take the job.

In terms of software:

All you need to get started is an Office package (Word, Excel, PowerPoint). Try to buy the newest version you can afford to avoid compatibility problems with your clients. You can buy and install a version for a single computer that can last several years or take up a subscription which is valid for several PCs, but will need to be renewed annually. The latter is more expensive so you will have to decide which solution best suits your circumstances.

Do you need to buy a CAT tool?

A Computer Assisted Translation (CAT) tool is a software programme which supports and facilitates the translation process – used to ensure speed, quality and consistency during the translation process. Some of the most popular brands on the market are Trados, Wordfast and MemoQ although translators frequently recommend others too. It is not necessary to have this kind of software when you are just starting out, especially if you don't know at this stage whether you are going to have a lot of repeat business from the same client or area of work. Buying a CAT tool is an investment and this is also to be taken into consideration as these products cost several hundred pounds. If you think a CAT tool would be useful, you can opt for a free trial before committing yourself financially and try out a few different systems before deciding which one you are most comfortable with. As part of your research, you can search for tutorials on YouTube which will take you through the process of using a CAT tool step-by-step. Proz also offers free demonstrations as part of events such as their virtual conference day, which takes place annually. On such occasions, they also offer translators the chance to purchase CAT tools at a reduced rate through group discounts.

Translation Memory Systems

A translation memory is a database which continually captures your translations as you work so that you can call on previous texts for future use. That way if the same sentence or phrase comes up in another document, you don't have to translate it again. The more you build up your translation memory, the faster you can translate subsequent files, enabling you to take on more projects and increase your revenue.

Using SDL Trados Studio as an example, you would open the source file and apply the translation memory so that any "100% matches" (identical matches) or "fuzzy matches" (similar, but not identical matches) within the text are instantly extracted and placed within the target file.

As you work through the source file, the "matches" suggested by the translation memory can be either accepted or overridden with new alternatives. If a translation unit is manually updated, then it is stored within the translation memory for future use as well as for repetition in the current text. In a similar way, all segments in the target file without a "match" would be translated manually and then automatically added to the translation memory.

When working for larger companies in particular, you might receive a document to translate that has been matched to a translation memory system. Companies using this type of system will apply different rates per 1,000 words depending on the level of matched text. For example I get paid my full rate for 100% new text, two thirds of my rate for a fuzzy match and a third for identical text. I must say that I was concerned about agreeing to these terms at first but I have found that it works and I am no worse for it.

Do you need professional indemnity Insurance?

The answer is: it depends. If you work through agencies, the consensus is that generally you do not need indemnity insurance as you are covered through the agency policy. If you work directly for clients who have offices in several countries and you know that your translations will be sent to the relevant office to be checked, then again, you shouldn't need insurance cover, if you ensure that the final version will be approved by the client. The example often mentioned to justify taking up insurance is the case where you translate a text which is due to be printed in large numbers. If a mistake is discovered after the document has been printed, the company you did the translation for could be entitled to ask you for compensation which can be substantial depending on the loss suffered. Whether to get insurance or not is a personal decision based on how you feel and on your circumstances. I took up some insurance cover when I started out but I didn't renew it after 2 or 3 years and I haven't felt the need to have it ever since. I believe it is quite rare for a client to claim compensation against a translator. Some translators might use the fact that they are insured as an additional selling point, however it could be perceived by some clients as an open invitation to claim some compensation! In summary, this is a personal choice.

CONCLUSION

Having your own business requires you to work and think differently to when you were employed. You need procedures in place to ensure things run properly and to pay attention to details without losing sight of the big picture. One way to let your business flourish is to protect it as much as possible against various threats and this is discussed in Chapter 11. Another way is to allow it to grow by expanding your services and this is the subject of the next chapter.

Chapter 10

OTHER LANGUAGE-BASED SERVICES

Translation is a gateway to many other language-based skills and opportunities to develop both yourself and your business. Here are the most common for you to consider.

Editing

Editing is the process of reviewing a translated document in detail in order to check and, when need be, improve the accuracy, flow and readability of language. Editing ensures that correct terminology has been used and involves rewriting sentences and even paragraphs to make the text clearer. To offer editing as a service, you need an extensive knowledge of the source and target language and you would normally only edit a text in your mother tongue.

An editor normally recommends changes but does not implement them. This is because, when there are errors, it is usually up to the original translator to correct their own mistakes and assess suggestions.

Editing can be paid either by the hour or by the word. When you charge by the hour, rates for editing should be equivalent to the hourly rate you would charge for translation. If charged by the word, this service should be charged at around half the rate for translation. Typically the net amount earned is broadly the same whichever method is applied. Personally I prefer to be paid an hourly rate for editing as all jobs differ in difficulty. That way you know that no matter how tough a job is, you will always be properly rewarded for the time you spend. Remember to always reconfirm the exact description of your services and your rate in writing to the client.

TOP TIP

Take a good look at the text before accepting an editing job as some translations are of such poor quality that it actually requires more work to edit the text than it would have required to do a fresh translation. If you find that this is the case, notify the client immediately and let them know that it will cost more to edit, or offer to translate it again. The alternative is to turn the job down. Remember you are in business and the work you take on has to be worth your time. So once again: assess carefully before accepting editing work.

Proofreading

Proofreading is the process of correcting grammatical, spelling, typographical and syntax errors in a document. It is more exhaustive than simply using a spell check function, which can miss things out or make incorrect suggestions. A proofreader must ensure zero grammatical errors after a document has been edited. The meaning of words and terminology doesn't need to be checked (that is part of the editing process). Therefore, the use of a dictionary is necessary only to check spelling and conjugation.

Again, my personal preference with proofreading is to be paid by the hour.

Localisation

Language localisation is the process of adapting a text that has already been translated to suit a specific country or region. It involves applying comprehensive knowledge of the target culture in order to correctly adapt the text to local needs, context and references.

Localisation is done for regions or countries where people speak different languages or where the same language is spoken with different idioms, for instance, different dialects of Spanish, are spoken in Spain and in Latin America.

Localisation can be summarised as changing the content of any document or information to make it work for a different geographical location.

Transcreation

Transcreation involves adapting a message from one language to another, while maintaining its intent, style, tone and context. It should evoke the same emotions and carry the same implications in the target language as it does in the source language. It is used a lot in global marketing and advertising campaigns for products which are sold in many countries. One example that springs to mind is a certain slogan by L'Oréal. The transcreation process ensures that images used within a creative message are suitable for the local target market.

Adaptation

Adaptation is the process of changing a text to ensure it is suitable for its target audience. It focuses on how the audience will read the text.

An adapted text can be phrased differently from its original version, since each word is strategically thought through and researched in order to create an effect on the reader. Its purpose is to engage your audience and create an impact on the reader, for example through a call-to-action. Adaptation makes a text more professional by adopting the right level of language and phrasing ideas in an elegant and sophisticated manner when any other option would be unacceptable. In order to do adaptation, you need to know your target audience very well and judge accurately how to phrase a text in order to have the desired effect.

Transcription

Transcription consists of creating a written record of audio or video soundtrack. It converts speech into a written or electronic text document. There are different variations of this service, all of which result in a text document containing the speech or dialogue from the source audio or video file.

Here again, I think the best way to charge is on an hourly basis.

Subtitling

Subtitling foreign language film and television is a difficult task because subtitles are so limited in space and time. Therefore the content of the dialogue has to be cut down to fit in the subtitles. Furthermore, the content has to be translated and the subtitles have to be 'spotted' or timed carefully to match the dialogue. When you translate into a language that takes more space than the source language (for instance from English into German) this is a real challenge as it requires writing very concisely without any loss of information.

Subtitling is a specialist service and you should be aware of the time required and investigate fully before taking on such work.

Interpreting

Although interpreting requires very different skills from translating, you might be asked occasionally by a client to step in and do some interpreting for them, especially if, as a translator, you have an in depth knowledge of the company and the specialist subject to be discussed. For some clients, it is a natural extension of their language service requirements and they want a native speaker they know and trust to take part in a conference call, Skype meeting or attend a meeting in person. This can be a great opportunity to further strengthen your relationship with that particular client. I have been asked to do some interpreting on several occasions and I have enjoyed the challenge of facilitating communication between the parties in different ways to my usual work, whilst still using my language skills and knowledge. If you find that you enjoy this kind of work and would like to offer interpreting as a service, I would recommend getting a recognised qualification through a professional body such as the Institute of Translation and Interpreting. You will have to decide whether you want to qualify in simultaneous or consecutive interpreting and what market you want to target (the police force, hospitals, business conferences). A premium hourly or daily rate should be charged as well as travelling and other related expenses.

Whatever the service, pay attention to approvals and sign off

A final note especially relating to these services is to ensure that the client knows they are responsible for the content of the final document. I know that all the clients I work with, whether agency or direct, ensure that a native speaker within their organisation reads and signs off a final version. If the client wants you to be responsible because they don't have the resources for the final check, then it is advisable to be very clear on the terms and conditions under which you are providing your services and consider professional indemnity insurance.

CONCLUSION

These skills can't be improvised and you need to work on them before you can offer them as a service. However, it is worth looking through the list and thinking now about other skills you might want to offer in the future and working to learn them when you have some gaps in your working day or year. For some, training courses are available for anyone who wishes to become proficient, broaden their offering and add some diversity to their work.

In the next chapter, I will be talking about ways to protect and grow your business once you are established and some issues to watch out for in order to give yourself the best chance to succeed.

Chapter 11

FROM EMPLOYEE TO ENTREPRENEUR: TAKING CHARGE AND GROWING YOUR BUSINESS

From employee to entrepreneur

Now you are working for yourself, the first thing to be aware of is that you are your own boss and that requires a different outlook and attitude.

There might be challenges ahead, but if you have a plan and you are determined, you will never need to feel helpless because you will always have something to do to help yourself on the way. Have a vision of your future self and bear in mind that every step you take towards that end goal will add to your skills and experience and help you become what you have envisioned.

Take a realistic look at yourself and establish what your strengths and weaknesses are. If you need to get better in certain areas, take action. You might feel that all you are doing for the time being is working hard and incurring expenses in the process but developing yourself will add value to your services and people will pay for those skills when you are ready.

Does the idea of being your own boss feel daunting?

It is important to have confidence in yourself and your skills, however this is hard to maintain when you feel that your experience is limited. So what can you do to help yourself?

- Take a different perspective on your situation. Think of your experience more broadly than just work experience and focus on your skills and abilities. Agencies are looking for high calibre individuals and they will be able to see your potential through your profile, even if you are new to the profession.

- Make a conscious decision to be confident. Even if you don't feel so at first, the more you act that way, the more you will look the part and the more it will become real.

- Try to communicate your passion and your enthusiasm. Demonstrate your love of languages, think about the wonderful things they have enabled you to experience.
- If you have an idea but you feel out of your depth, give it a go anyway. Taking risks is part of growing and acquiring experience.
- Stay positive. Avoid negative language and thoughts and surround yourself with positive people. Optimism is catching.
- Be patient with yourself. Don't beat yourself up if things don't work out at first. And remember that there is no such thing as perfection; everyone has something they can improve on.
- Above all, take action. Everything you do to move yourself towards your goal will increase your confidence and belief in your ability.

  Adding to your skills doesn't necessarily involve months of study. Nowadays you can find a lot of courses online, some of them free, to add to your credentials. Treat the journey as an adventure. It might feel like a marathon, but it can be enjoyable as long as you see yourself in full control and you keep the conviction that you will get there. When you reach your goal, you will be a different person in that you will be more competitive, more confident and more professional.

Growing your business

Once you have got some work and you begin to grow more confident in your skills and ability to get more, you can focus on expanding your business. You have found out what works best for you in terms of marketing yourself and you know the type of translation work you would like to concentrate on. Your main priority is still to increase your income by taking on more assignments, however you can picture yourself in the future running a proper business and it is worth starting to plan for this. Visualising this next phase in your career will give you an extra incentive to work harder and realise your goal.

Sometimes you develop an area of expertise through whatever opportunities are available to you as you pick up work. For example, I have been doing a lot of translation for the last 12 years for clients in the printing and packaging industry. This is not necessarily an industry I would have thought of looking into, however, having developed an expertise in that area, I would be pleased to take on more work from companies in that sector as I feel familiar and confident with the subject matter.

You have now established that you enjoy working as a freelance translator and this is what you want to be doing for the foreseeable future. Now is the time to use any gaps in your working week to plan for the future. Your main aims are to

- **manage risks**
- **nurture your existing business**
- **develop new business**

1) MANAGING RISK

Once your business has grown to a certain level, it becomes a valuable asset which you need to protect. You have invested time, money and effort in getting where you are and you do not want to jeopardise your achievement. There are several steps to consider implementing in order to stay safe:

Consider your client base

Set some funds aside to cover eventualities such as:

- losing your biggest client. Businesses change and evolve all the time and there might be many reasons why a client will cease to use your services, such as restructuring, a change in management, cost reduction measures, a merger with another company. If your income depends for a large part on a single client this puts you in a vulnerable position. It is always advisable to try and diversify your client base by working not only for different companies, but also for different industries and even for customers in different countries;

- not being able to work for a while due to ill health. As soon as you can, set some money aside in case you need to support yourself while you are out of work. If you work in the UK, your national insurance contributions give you some social security benefits. Find out what you would be entitled to by contacting your local job centre. If you live outside the UK, check which benefits would be available to you in your country of residence. That way you will know whether the level of cover is sufficient or whether you should have additional provisions in place;

- a fall in the translation work available due to an economic downturn. Economic cycles are a fact of life and you should be prepared for the eventuality that there might be changes in the macroeconomic environment which will affect you. In the case of economic influences, some countries or even sectors are affected differently at any one time and this is why it is good to diversify your sources of work and even have clients in different currency zones.

To protect yourself against the risk of a drop in your income whatever the reason, it is advisable to save a portion of your earnings as soon as you can or have alternative provisions in place to cope with any unforeseen circumstances. Generally speaking, it is accepted that you should have reserves equivalent to 4 months of outgoings to tie you over.

Credit control

One way of safeguarding your income is to ensure that you get paid for your work.

Take a look at your client list: do you trust them all to always pay you? Do you happen to know if some of them are in a vulnerable position? If you are not entirely sure that you will be paid in full for your work, you might not want to do a large job that involves a week's work or more. Not only would you not have an income for the time spent on the job, but you would be missing out on other opportunities by being unavailable to others. If you have a large document which can be divided into chunks, you can ask to be paid in stages. A few years ago, I asked an agency to take me off their translators' list because getting paid was always a problem. I think they were facing financial difficulties; payments were always delayed and I often received them in small instalments after of lot of chasing. Although I didn't lose any money, it was not worth the time or the worry and I decided not to work for them again.

A word of warning: Beware of scammers!

Scams are a fact of life and you are better off knowing about them in order to protect yourself and avoid a bad experience. Some scammers specifically target translators and this section aims to make you aware of that fact and to help you recognise the situation should you ever get confronted with the problem.

There are several types of scammers:

- those who are trying to steal your CV and impersonate you (hence my advice in Chapter 8 to always send your CV in a PDF format)

- those who give you work but never send any payment and disappear once you have sent your translation

- those who try to steal money through various schemes reminiscent of more well-known scams (the stranded traveller asking for help to get back home, etc.) which usually involves persuading you to part with money upfront.

When approached by a prospective client, ask yourself how they got hold of your details and try and ascertain their credibility and reputation. Don't feel that you are being unreasonable, it is not only legitimate but also good business practice to want to know who you are dealing with before deciding if you can trust them.

If you are contacted by an agency, check their e-mail address. Although it is perfectly acceptable for a freelance translator to have an e-mail address based on a free e-mail provider such as Gmail or Hotmail, a reputable agency should have an e-mail address based on its domain name which usually includes their trading name.

However, checking this alone is no guarantee that they are genuine: some more sophisticated scammers can copy real agencies' websites and it is hard sometimes to spot the difference between a fake and a genuine website unless you pay attention to the smallest details. If they appear to be a reputable agency, do a separate search through Google and see if their domain name is different in any way to the one you found through that separate search. Sometimes the only way to tell they are fake is through details in their domain name where for example they replace a small symbol by another such as a dash by an underscore, or words get separated by a dot instead of being written in a single word or vice versa. Therefore you must be particularly vigilant.

What you can do if you are suspicious:

- Carry out some basic checks as a matter of principle on anyone new who contacts you to offer you a job until you are satisfied that they can be trusted.

- Check their e-mail address and domain name.

- Ask other translators on forums if anyone has any experience of working with them.

- Do an internet search to see if there is any information about them and their activity.

- Check on www.translators-scammers.com to see if they are listed.

- If you are a member of Proz, check the Blue Board.

- If you decide to accept a job, make sure it is a small job to start with in order to test them. If they turn out to be disappointing, you won't have lost much and if they are genuine, you will have won a new client.

- Always ask for a purchase order number and written confirmation of their order before you get started.

- If you are contacted by someone who you recognise to be a scammer, ignore them and report them to others but don't respond to them directly. Just like telephone scammers, there are too many of them and it is important not to engage with them.

- Stay alert and in touch with other translators. New scams come through all the time and some are very clever and sophisticated so anyone can fall for them. The more informed you are, the better protected you will be.

Finally, if you encounter the type of scammer who contacts translators with a fake job offer in order to steal money from them, you will know you are dealing with a fraudster because there are always conditions attached, usually in the form of a payment: you will be required to either pay some bogus administration or legal fees based on a fictitious scenario or invest in a special software package in order to get a large amount of work.

The most insidious case is where a scammer offers you a job with an upfront payment by cheque in order to gain your trust. Invariably, the amount sent is much larger than what was agreed between you and you then get asked, for the sake of simplicity, to cash in the cheque and just send the difference back. Even if the cheque appears genuine and gets accepted by your bank, it will bounce at a later date and if in the meantime you have sent the difference back, you will have lost your money. Therefore be clear that you should never have to make a payment to anyone in order to get a job, regardless how convincing the reason might sound.

It is worth remembering the following two rules about scammers in order to stay safe:

- Never, ever make any payment or incur any expenses in order to get a specific job

- Don't be blinded by your desire to find work. If something looks too appealing to be true, it probably is.

2) NURTURING YOUR EXISTING BUSINESS

Once you have won your first few customers, your priority will be to keep them and strengthen your relationship with them. There are simple steps you can take:

- Keep in touch on a regular basis through short messages, letting them know your availability and giving relevant updates about your profile. This helps remind your contact that you are around.

- Be an active member of a community of translators. Join a forum or another group and ask for advice or give advice, contribute to blogs, initiate discussions and share your experience.

- Concentrate on being visible: how do others perceive you and your business? Are you easy to find? Do you sound and look professional through your profile, your job applications, your marketing literature, etc.? What is your range of expertise? Do you offer other services aside from translation?

- Would your clients be ready to refer you to other departments in their organisation?

- Would your clients be willing to recommend you to external contacts?

3) DEVELOPING NEW BUSINESS

When you reach a steady volume of work, your focus will shift to growing and stabilising your business. Your priorities will change again and you will concentrate more on acquiring new clients.

Keep up to date with trends and changes, find out what is most in demand, what skills, services or specialisms are most sought after. This is one way of staying involved and challenging yourself.

The bottom line is to be proactive. The alternative would be to settle down at a level which you find comfortable and stop learning or improving. There have been a lot of changes in the translation industry in the last 10 years and it is important to adapt to those changes in order to stay competitive. Think of investing in yourself in order to further increase your income. This could take several forms:

Embrace technology

Update your software packages. Check that the versions you are using are not dated as that creates problems when you send and receive files from clients.

Do not ignore technology. Identify what investment would be useful to develop your business and give yourself the means to achieve growth. Investigate and decide whether it would be worth purchasing a CAT tool. If this is the right thing for you, you must not view it as an expenditure but as an investment which should pay for itself in a relatively short period of time.

Be open to new language opportunities, especially those driven by advances in technology. In a fast developing world, new areas of work and new specialist subjects emerge all the time. Keep abreast of changes and dedicate some time to a few subjects you are interested in.

Sign up for courses

Investing in yourself doesn't always mean spending money: there are a lot of free courses you can benefit from. The effect of this learning might not immediately lead to new work and new income, but if there are specialist subjects you are interested in, it is worth nurturing your interest and learning something useful and exciting for your career and the future.

You can sign up to free online courses on a variety of subjects, for example through MOOCs (Massively Open Online Courses) which offer topics such as computer science, humanities and business to name but a few. These are free online courses from top universities. Coursera, Edx and Canvas Network are also some of the better-known providers of such courses.

Diversify your client base

Although it is easier to find work through agencies when you get started and have relatively little experience, you should stay open to the possibility of having direct clients too.

Diversify your skills

Consider broadening your offering by adding other services to your list. There are many other services freelance translators frequently offer alongside translation such as editing, proofreading, transcreation, interpreting (see Chapter 10).

Get your pricing policy right

One way of strengthening your business is to get your pricing policy right. As a newcomer, it is tempting to start on a low rate but after a while it is advisable to re-evaluate what you are charging and check that your rate is not too low for the work that you do.

When you start receiving regular work and becoming expert in your field, you no longer feel you have to accept whatever you get offered. The balance starts shifting in your favour and you grow confident enough to start negotiating a better deal for yourself. Obviously, you need to be very aware of what others with similar skills are charging to define your own rates. You can sound out one or two clients and see what their reaction is before deciding to apply an increase more broadly.

TOP TIP

You will not necessarily have the same rate for everyone and every document you translate: even now, I have different rates for different customers. This depends on several things:

- the level of expertise involved
- how much work there is outside the actual translation work
- the industry sector
- your experience and your relationship with your client company

It is a good idea to revise your rates fairly regularly and apply small increases rather than a higher rise at once. If your client values you, they won't mind a modest annual increase and you have another year to impress them and make yourself indispensable!

Have a business plan

Having a business plan is useful, if not essential. As you are most probably a sole trader, it can be fairly quick to draw up and the exercise makes you think about what exactly you want from your business, what your expectations are, what direction you want to take, what your core values are and what you should focus on. It is tempting to think that these things are obvious and you know them all. However, writing down your goals will help you focus on what you need to achieve. Suddenly, you realise that some of them require some thinking through and adapting to your circumstances.

At least once a year, look at your business and set clear targets. You should also write down what you need to renew or acquire in terms of equipment, tools and training. It is important to get the balance right between earning an income and developing your business and a plan will help you achieve that.

A business plan saves you from wasting time, energy and money trying several different avenues at random. It helps you feel more confident and in control because you have a clearer idea of the direction you are taking and can guide how you present your business, which clients to approach and how. Revert back to your plan from time to time, check your progress, remind yourself of your main goals and ask yourself some questions: Has your focus changed? Is there something you have lost sight of? Is there anything you've neglected or not been able to achieve? Have you come across anything that inspires new marketing ideas?

CONCLUSION

You are now in charge of generating your own income and you need to be creative and resourceful in the process. Once you are clear about this, you immediately start to feel differently about the situation, i.e. less vulnerable and more in control. Suddenly, instead of hoping that someone will give you a job, you will be proactive in taking steps towards generating your future income. This is what companies of all sizes do every day. If you were previously employed, this is what your boss had to worry about while you were concentrating on doing your job. Now you have put yourself in the top position and that is both thrilling and energising.

The following pages serve to summarise a few important pieces of advice in order to make the best of your newly chosen profession and to encourage you to embrace what lies ahead with enthusiasm. You are where you wanted to be, so from now on it's up to you how far you want to take it. I hope you have enjoyed the learning so far and that you are looking forward to the journey ahead of you.

Chapter 12

PUT YOURSELF FIRST: CONCLUDING THOUGHTS BEFORE YOU GET GOING

The future of your business rests entirely on you and it is essential to look after yourself in order to look after your business.

Have a healthy lifestyle

In Chapter 6 I highlighted the fact that working as a freelance translator gives you advantages in terms of flexibility and lifestyle and it is important to make the most of these.

Give yourself the most favourable routine in order to be as alert and productive as you can. Allow yourself some relaxing activities to manage stress, surround yourself with positive people who are bright and enthusiastic, read biographies of people who inspire you.

Pay attention to your stress levels. When you need a real break or change of scenery, why not go out for a walk or a run. Physical exercise enables you to relax, recharge your batteries and put things in perspective.

Think about job satisfaction

What keeps you motivated? What do you find rewarding about your job? Are your customers grateful for your support? Do you see the results and effect of your work helping your clients communicate effectively with their own customers?

Talk about your business with enthusiasm, pay attention to people's reactions. It will make you realise the value of what you have achieved so far and see the exciting prospect of what else you are striving for.

Keep learning

As in many other professions, freelance translators need to keep up to date with new working methods, tools and techniques. There are numerous activities available to you, many of which can be pursued online from your desk. Here is a reminder of just a few options:

- Reading foreign language newspapers and professional publications
- Listening to relevant radio programmes
- Making use of online tutorials and e-learning
- Signing up to courses organised by universities
- Getting involved, for example volunteering at events which support the translation industry
- Taking part in webinars, conferences, lectures and workshops organised by professional bodies
- Writing (blogs, book reviews, articles, etc.)

Although all worthwhile in themselves, you can also record all activities which contribute to your continuous professional development. This helps you maintain high professional standards and show an agency or direct client evidence of your efforts. For more information on the subject, visit www.cpdstandards.com.

CONCLUSION

When you have reached a level where you generate a regular income from your translation work, your confidence and your sense of enjoyment grow. Of course, you will keep on working just as hard but it will feel different because you are protecting, nurturing and growing something you have created. Where you take it from here and how far you go is up to you. No matter what stage you are at in your career, there is always scope for acquiring new knowledge, learning new skills and establishing new relationships. This is both humbling and exciting.

If you feel that you still have a long way to go before reaching your goal, bear in mind that all progress will come from the initiatives that you will take. Therefore the one thing to remember is to be constantly proactive. This doesn't necessarily need to be time consuming and difficult though, in fact it is important to strike a balance and build in some fun and rewarding activities as well in order to keep yourself motivated.

Once established, many freelance translators wish to give something back in order to help others on their way. They want to support a professional community which helped them throughout their career so it can perpetuate itself and reach out to many more newcomers. Giving back can take many forms, for example teaching, mentoring, volunteering at translators' events as well as speaking at conferences or simply giving advice on forums or through a column in a professional publication.

The value of language and quality communication

Time to sum up

I hope that this book has painted a realistic picture of the journey to building a career as a freelance translator. I also hope to have inspired you to embark on what I believe is a relevant, interesting and profitable path. I trust you have found some inspiration, both from reinforcement of ideas you already had and from new ideas to try and sustain you.

To finish, a note on the value of language and quality communication which is for me very important, along with all the other motivations of my profession mentioned in this book. As a freelance translator you will be challenged to find the perfect word, phrase, alliteration, ... It is both thrilling and satisfying when you get it just right. So above all, look for that challenge, enjoy the work. You will explore topics and subjects you have never come across before, work with some great people and set yourself up to take control of your work-life balance.

I wish you happy translating!

USEFUL WEBSITES

Language related organisations

www.atc.org.uk
www.ciol.org.uk
www.iti.org.uk

Distance courses for the CIOL Diploma in Translation

www.city.ac.uk/translation
www.liverpoolcitycollege.com
London Metropolitan University – l.kaczmarek@londonmet.ac.uk
www.translator-training.com
www.ja-cie-naucze.com

Membership based websites

www.proz.com
www.traduguide.com
www.translationdirectory.com
www.translatorsbase.com
www.translatorscafe.com

Outsourcers

www.fivver.com
www.studentgems.com
www.upwork.com

Online dictionaries and translation tools

www.en.pons.com
www.lexicool.com
www.linguee.com
www.logosdictionary.org
www.reverso.net
www.wordreference.com

CV writing

www.thewritestuff.co.uk

Setting up your own business

www.gov.uk/set-up-business-uk/overview
www.gov.uk/set-up-sole-trader/overview
www.gov.uk/apply-national-insurance-number

Website creation

www.wordpress.com

Other

www.cpdstandards.com
www.languageshowlive.co.uk
www.translators-scammers.com